Mathias Albert, Hauke Brunkhorst, Iver B. Neumann, Stephan Stetter
The Social Evolution of World Politics

Political Science | Volume 143

Mathias Albert, born in 1967, is a professor of political science at Universität Bielefeld. He specializes in the history and sociology of world politics, youth research, and polar politics.

Hauke Brunkhorst, born in 1945, is a senior professor of sociology at Europa-Universität Flensburg. He has published widely in social and legal philosophy as well as on the sociology and evolution/revolution of law and constitutions.

Iver B. Neumann, born in 1959, is a political scientist and social anthropologist and director of the Fridtjof Nansen Institute in Oslo. He specializes in the history and pre-history of world politics as well as on contemporary affairs, particularly in relation to Russia.

Stephan Stetter, born in 1972, is a professor of international politics and conflict studies at the Universität der Bundeswehr München. His main research interests are the history and sociology of world politics as well as Middle Eastern politics and EU foreign affairs.

Mathias Albert, Hauke Brunkhorst, Iver B. Neumann, Stephan Stetter
The Social Evolution of World Politics

[transcript]

Bibliographic information published by the Deutsche Nationalbibliothek
The Deutsche Nationalbibliothek lists this publication in the Deutsche Nationalbibliografie; detailed bibliographic data are available in the Internet at http://dnb.d-nb.de

This work is licensed under the Creative Commons Attribution 4.0 (BY) license, which means that the text may be remixed, transformed and built upon and be copied and redistributed in any medium or format even commercially, provided credit is given to the author.
Creative Commons license terms for re-use do not apply to any content (such as graphs, figures, photos, excerpts, etc.) not original to the Open Access publication and further permission may be required from the rights holder. The obligation to research and clear permission lies solely with the party re-using the material.

First published in 2023 by transcript Verlag, Bielefeld
© **Mathias Albert, Hauke Brunkhorst, Iver B. Neumann, Stephan Stetter**

Cover layout: Maria Arndt, Bielefeld
Printed by: Majuskel Medienproduktion GmbH, Wetzlar
https://doi.org/10.14361/9783839465271
Print-ISBN: 978-3-8376-6527-7
PDF-ISBN: 978-3-8394-6527-1
ISSN of series: 2702-9050
eISSN of series: 2702-9069

Printed on permanent acid-free text paper.

I ain't getting old, I'm evolving – Keith Richards

Contents

Acknowledgements 9

1 Introduction: 'Deep history' for understanding world politics 11
1.1 Long-term change in IR 15
1.2 Plan of the book 18

2 The coevolution of society and evolutionary theory
 through four Axial Ages 23
2.1 Pre-Axial segmentary societies and the First Axial Age:
 Learning and institutionalizing equality and liberty, ca.
 100,000-3500 BCE 24
2.2 The Second Axial Age or the age of counter-present
 theorizing of stratified/imperial class societies and the
 memory of universalism, ca. 800-200 BCE 27
2.3 The Third Axial Age: Early functional differentiation and
 the turn to immanence-theorizing societal change, ca. 1000-1750 32
2.4 The Fourth Axial Age: The planetary age of global
 constitutionalism and explicit social evolutionary
 theorizing, ca. 1750-present 37

3 Contemporary social evolution and social evolutionary theories ... 49

3.1 Social evolution and theories of society 49
3.2 Cognitive and normative evolution: Learning and unlearning 63
3.3 Core evolutionary concepts: Autonomization,
    hierarchical complexity and coevolution 74
3.4 Existing approaches to evolution in IR 79

4 Evolutionary trajectories in world politics 91
4.1 Forms of organizing political authority
    in the emergence and transformation
    of a modern system of world politics 91
4.2 The restabilization of world politics and peacebuilding 105
4.3 The evolution of world politics through the practice of diplomacy ... 124

5 Social evolution and knowing world politics 139

References 147

Acknowledgements

We would like to thank all those who have provided us over the years with valuable comments on parts of this project, which brought us together at various conferences and workshops, most notably at three author retreats in Bayrischzell, Niederbreitenbach and Neuastenberg. We would particularly like to thank Emanuel Adler for the extensive feedback that he gave on an earlier and much shorter version of the text. Jan Koslowski and Nathalie Stumpf have supported this work as student assistants. Invaluable help on the language has come from Stephen Curtis.

We gratefully acknowledge the financial support for this project that we received from the University of the Bundeswehr Munich and Bielefeld University. We are also very grateful for support for the publication costs provided by the Open Access Publication Fund of Bielefeld University and the Deutsche Forschungsgemeinschaft (DFG).

1 Introduction: 'Deep history' for understanding world politics

The present book proposes a framework for understanding long-term change in world politics in terms of social evolution. 'Change' deliberately includes the very emergence of world politics as a recognizable realm in its own right within the social world and its constant transformation thereafter. In order to provide such a framework, this book offers a condensed, yet quite far-reaching, reading of what it means to understand change in the social, and therefore also the political, world in terms of evolution, as well as several empirical applications from the realm of world politics. It is written on the premise that understanding social evolutionary processes is central to understanding historical change. Yet, there is a difference between the historical and sociological approaches to social evolution. While we maintain that the approaches do not necessarily stand in mutually exclusive opposition to each other, evolutionary accounts are *not* compatible with some understandings of history, particularly those, based on a philosophy of history, that assign meaning to history itself (and therefore come with, for example, underlying eschatological or teleological motives).

Understanding long-term change in world politics in terms of social evolution is, in one respect, a rather simple exercise: it allows historical change to be reconstructed in accordance with the sequence that underlies *all* kinds of evolution (i.e., not only social but also natural evolution): variation, selection and restabilization. In another respect, though, it makes this reconstruction extremely complex. It obliges one to see change in a broad societal context, accounting for various timescales, taking the contingency of change and of social structures fully into account and emphasizing the non-synchronized evolution of linked, but at the same time diverse, social systems. It requires one, in other words, to ensure that due attention is paid to both the indeterminacy inherent in evolution and its ontological openness. In such a perspective, it makes little sense to posit that something like an 'international system' exists, only to then ask how that system evolves independently. Rather, although specific systems, fields, milieus and other realms within the social world have to be analysed according to their individual characteristics, which can only be asserted and observed on the basis of some specific delimitation from the rest of the social world, 'delimitation' here does not mean outright separation. It points instead to the fact that there is an ongoing and historically very specific process that produces distinctiveness through a continuous delineation of differences. It is in this broad sense that we use the notion of 'world politics', thus underlining the fact that politics-between-polities is a social realm that has the directly or indirectly accessible social world of each era as its spatial 'horizon', and its imaginaries of pasts, presents and futures as its temporal horizons. As a result, we always need to account for how – in historically changing ways – world politics changes while being embedded in a wider social environment that constitutes the spatial and temporal boundary condition for its evolution; and this embedding, in turn, requires that the way in which cross-polity politics came to appear as a distinct realm within that environment (with, for example, specific underlying notions of power and specific forms of organizing political authority) should be accounted for. While every analysis necessarily contains a reduction of the world's complexity, we posit that it might very possibly be an excessive decomplexification of the different evolutionary trajectories of different systems operating on different timescales and at different speeds. This led, at least in part, to the temporal 'presentism' and conceptual 'Eurocentrism' in the academic field of International Relations (IR), a decomplexification that, not least, may have expressed itself in the wholesale state of 'being surprised' by things like the end of the Cold War or the outbreak of the Russia–Ukraine War – thus not taking sufficient account of

1 Introduction: 'Deep history' for understanding world politics 13

both the historicity of world politics (its temporal dimension) and its already always global conceptual anchoring.

While we will address this point in more detail later, it is important to highlight here that this present study is certainly not the first to try and use evolutionary theory in the analysis of world politics broadly understood. However, it is deliberately set apart from most other such attempts, which, more often than not, are built on a category mistake: it is simply and plainly wrong to take theories of natural evolution and apply them directly to the analysis of change in the social world. The fundamental form of evolution needs to be read and 'filtered' through theories of society/sociological theories if it is to be able to account both for the specific conditions of social evolution (for example, that the evolving units in this case are not genes but, as we highlight below, communications) and for some of the features specific to evolution in the social world, in particular the possibilities of evolutionary learning (and unlearning). All this happens in the world beyond genes, which is a world in which natural evolution takes not place.[1] We thus define society as being constituted by and through communications (and whatever is linked to them, discourse, etc.). Communication as sense-making signals (including non-verbal communication) are what distinguishes human society from other realms of evolution (nature, other species, etc). Natural evolution or events in the non-social world (e.g. in animal societies) in that sense coevolve with social evolution, e.g. when a new virus pops up (and people deal with a pandemic), dogs and cats make themselves at home (and are turned into pets), ice sheets melt (forcing people to move from coastal regions), or asteroids are passing

---

1 As we will discuss further below, the situation with cognitive evolution (i.e., the evolution of individual psychological meaning-processing systems – viz. consciousness – as prominently applied by Adler (2019) to the world of IR) is a bit more complex. In another respect, although we are aware of discussions about possible cultural evolution in a cosmic context (i.e., one not limited to planet Earth), we only deal with theories of social evolution in what thus far empirically has remained a world society limited to this planet (cf. Dick and Lupisella 2009; Deudney 2020).

by Earth (prompting doomsday scenarios and interception experiments), but they are not themselves part of a communication-based social world and its distinct realms, such as world politics. Our book can draw from a distinct intellectual tradition here. In varying forms – and most often refraining from use of the term 'evolution' though engaging in evolution-related thinking nonetheless – such a social evolutionary understanding of change is present in much of the 'classical' tradition of sociology broadly conceived, from Spencer via Marx to Durkheim and Weber. Even more than that, as we show in detail below, it has figured prominently in reflections on the human social condition since time immemorial and shaped intellectual preoccupations with the course of history and the possibilities and conditions of change since at least the major 'philosophical' revolution of the Second Axial Age. For the coiner of the phrase, Karl Jaspers (1949), that was actually the First Axial Age, a concept further developed from a social science perspective by Assmann (2018). However, as we will come back to below, when Jaspers was writing in the 1940s, much less was known about social life in the fourth and third millennia BCE than we know now. We shall therefore have to revise Jaspers slightly by postulating that a First Axial Age took place at that time.

Going back to modernity and what sociological classics have argued, we built our argument in particular on the observation that social evolution is also a noticeable component (now through explicit references) in some of the major comprehensive social theories of the twentieth century, namely Foucault's, Habermas's and Luhmann's readings of society – three theoretical perspectives that we draw on in particular in this book when setting out our sociological understanding of social evolution. We use these theories in a decidedly eclectic fashion in order to devise an analytical 'core' for analysing change in world politics in social evolutionary terms. By doing so, we also bring a cross-disciplinary perspective to the field of IR, the discipline that has traditionally claimed prime responsibility for analysing world politics. In addition, we bring to that discipline literatures, as well as readings of some literatures, that it has thus far chosen to ignore almost totally, even while actively engaging with some of the authors in question (in particular, Habermas and

Foucault, both of whom are widely, and we would argue wrongly, not understood to be evolution-theory scholars) or with different concepts of evolution. In fact, we find this ignorance to be so remarkable in what it says about the knowledge structure of IR as a discipline that we explicitly address it in the concluding chapter.

1.1 Long-term change in IR

Needless to say, even before it comes to social evolution, there is no denying that an important part of IR's remit is to account for longterm change and that this underpins the recent surge in historically oriented studies of world politics, or international systems more generally, during the nineteenth century, for instance, early modernity or even before the modern era.[2] This has helped to challenge the often sterile character of major IR theories presented in a specific post–World War II American tradition that aims to render similar the social and the natural worlds on the basis of quasi-objective laws. This focus on change pertains to all levels of the political, from relations between the rulers and the ruled (authority), via practices such as those pertaining to conflict, to institutions such as law and diplomacy (which are empirical applications that we tackle in the final quarter of the book). With the conspicuous exception of the neorealists, who see IR as a separate and transhistorical realm cut off from the social, most IR scholars would perceive ongoing longterm change as a characteristic of international systems. Given continuing large-scale changes in the natural preconditions for social and political life (e.g. the climate crisis) as well as in the structural

---

2 This recent 'surge' in historically oriented studies of world politics, very often (but not always) under the rubric of historical political sociology, arguably appears as a surge mainly because, for many years, an increasingly US-focused discipline took part in the widespread dehistoricization entailed by a 'mainstream' discursive field structured by the two 'neo'-poles (i.e., neorealism and neo-institutionalism) that displaced the more historically sensitive strands in the early (e.g. 'classical' realist) or non-U.S. (e.g. 'English School', continental) traditions of IR.

principles on which social and political life rests (e.g. the technological change underpinning contemporary globalization), analyses of long-term change are particularly apposite today.

While specific IR literatures exist that attempt to answer such questions, perhaps most pertinently theories of hegemonic change (e.g. Gilpin 1981; Thompson 2001) and comparative systems studies (e.g. Phillips and Sharman 2015), IR has been at one with other social sciences in turning to evolutionary theory for support in analysing long-term change. In its most basic – and also most problematic – form, this has involved scholars attempting to apply the principles of natural evolution directly to the social realm in a simple and effortless way (Johnson 2015; Thayer 2009). Given that there are no social equivalents to the two basic mechanisms on which natural evolution rests – natural selection that sees species adapt to specific biotopic niches, and sexual selection that sees evolutionary patterns grow out of patterns based on the choice of mating partners – such attempts are mistaken and bound to fail. Independently of how natural and how sexy world politics might appear to some observers, these are not the factors that shape this social system's evolution.

IR also sports a small but lively literature on cognitive evolution (e.g. Adler 2019; McDermott and Hatemi 2018). However, by focusing on cognition, which is by definition individual rather than social in nature, this literature deals with social change only indirectly, via the individual level (but see Mercer 2017). Cognitive evolutionary approaches are, therefore, at one with natural evolutionary approaches in trying to explain *social* change in terms of *non-social* factors. While this is methodologically dubious with respect to the practical analysis of specific problems where both cognitive and social learning play a role, analyses of social and cognitive evolution might usefully complement one other (see below, 3.2).

In this book we will present an alternative to these approaches. Building on a broad but somewhat subterranean tradition of social evolution in (mostly) continental European social theory, we will forge a social evolutionary approach to the study of IR, one that is self-reflexive in the sense that it includes the evolution of its own subject matter in its account. Our basic move is to take neither agents nor structures as the central unit of evolution, but to focus

1 Introduction: 'Deep history' for understanding world politics 17

on relations between agents, relations forged and shaped by communication signals (Emirbayer 1997). In this, we have been preceded by such luminaries as Foucault, Habermas and Luhmann, all of whose analyses flowed from a focus on relations – initially brought to the social sciences by Simmel – or, as we will show in greater detail below, units of communication and discourses in which such relations are embedded. In addition to the general methodological soundness of starting analyses of the social from 'social stuff' rather than biology, psychology or methodological individualism in the social sciences, such an approach has two further distinct advantages. Firstly, it allows for a direct focus on learning and unlearning, again at all levels of social life. What is in question here is not some unidirectional process that produces ever better goal-oriented action, but change, often radical change, affecting the practices and institutions of social life. This includes the distinct possibility of unlearning as well as learning: evolution is not inherently 'progressive' in accordance with some kind of normative criterion available from outside evolution (as would be the case if, for example, history was seen to move inevitably towards salvation). Social evolution can be judged as progressive (or regressive, for that matter) against normative criteria of what constitutes progress over a certain period of time – but then those normative criteria themselves need to be analysed in terms of their social evolution as temporary boundary conditions, conditioning the likelihoods of certain selections being made.

Secondly, the approach maintains a certain openness. We do not take for granted that certain agents (say states), structures (say anarchy) or even levels of analysis (say the international system) should be privileged a priori, but remain sensitive to how these factors change across time and space.

We see social evolution as a process that plays out in three phases, reflecting the formal sequencing of *all* evolution, social, natural or cognitive. At some point, a certain practice, institution or system will be characterized by fairly stable characteristics. Then (1) variation between these, born of resistance to the dominant way of doing things (a 'no' in the communication theory perspective we draw from) will be in evidence. This variation triggered by negations may grow, until (2) a selection of one variant occurs and something changes. There will then be (3) a restabilization of the practice, institution or entire system around the chosen variant, until change again sets in. It will make a difference which of these levels the process plays out on. Relations between coexisting evolutionary sequences of variation, selection and restabilization are also important if we want to analyse the trajectory of any one sequence. Finally, such processes will have different inherent temporalities and involve different constellations of variants; these may vary in number and depth of difference. An analysis of all these three factors taken together has the potential to account for long-term change both on the micro and macro levels and across phenomena.

1.2 Plan of the book

In this book we deliberately take the longer route to introducing the evolution of social evolution and theories of social evolution. We purposely avoid any shortcuts here in order to emphasize that social evolution is not something that can be reduced to some kind of specific modern or contemporary theory. The structural evolution of society/societies and the resultant emergence of (proto-)theories of social evolution are a pervasive feature of the history of humankind, and need to be deliberately reflected on in this context. Taking this longer way around is important for two reasons: firstly, it demonstrates how social evolution takes a separate path from natural evolution early on (in terms of human civilization); secondly, it shows that social evolution is a central motive within, and permeating much of, philosophical, theological, and later social scientific thought well before, and later alongside and after, the discovery of the figure of evolution. In such a broad perspective and long-term historical view, the evolution of evolutionary theory – from implicit accounts of social evolution theories *avant la lettre* to their modern self-reflexive equivalents – can roughly be divided into five phases in each of which quite a lot is happening, so to speak, in the evolution of evolutionary theory: the age of egalitarian (segmentary) societies (ca. 100,000-10,000 BCE); the First Axial Age, that of the first city-states (ca. 3500 BCE); the Second Axial Age, that of stratified/imperial class societies (ca.

800–200 BCE); the Third Axial Age, that of functional differentiation and the turn to immanence (ca. 1000–present); and the Fourth Axial Age (ca. 1750–present), which we call the planetary age of global constitutionalism.

Following this deliberately extended introduction to the evolution of evolutionary theory, we focus more concretely on the role that social evolutionary thinking plays in modern social theory. The starting point here is to highlight the fact that social evolutionary thinking is not in any way a novelty. On the contrary, it has not only been deeply engrained in thinking about the social world since antiquity (as addressed in the previous section), but has been articulated as explicit evolutionary theory since the inception of sociology as a discipline during the nineteenth century. In fact, it is as pervasive in many 'classical' theories of society as in many of the 'big' theories of the late twentieth century. However, no single theory of social evolution exists. What does exist is a core of perspectives on social evolution in the works of thinkers as different as, for example, Foucault and Luhmann. We do not identify this core as a basis of our further analyses by distilling an imagined common ground. Rather, our approach is a deliberately eclectic one – that is to say that we assemble a core of social evolutionary thought from pieces taken from the various theories in the full conviction that, when it comes to social theorizing on the basis of many social theories, eclecticism is the most productive way to go about it (so long, that is, as the eclecticism is based on a profound command of the theories in question, rather than on superficial and partial readings only). On this basis, we will proceed to briefly explicate the categorical difference between different forms of evolution, particularly between social and cognitive evolution, and the associated differences regarding the possibilities of cognitive and normative learning and unlearning. Processes of social learning and unlearning provide a key to understanding the long-term historical evolution of complex societies, or parts thereof. While they will always be linked to cognitive learning processes, they cannot be reduced to them, nor can they be deduced from them. This insight also leads us to a research programme of a general ontological openness when it comes to analysing social evolution. To paraphrase Luhmann, it is evolution that evolves: behind and beyond that, nothing is fixed. The three evolutionary 'core' concepts that lead us into, and will provide us with some guidance for, our empirical applications are then identified as autonomization, hierarchical complexity and coevolution. Before we turn to those applications, however, we will visit some of the extant applications of evolutionary thought in the discipline of International Relations. While we argue that Adler's concept of cognitive evolution in particular may ultimately be conjoined with a social evolution approach when it comes to specific analytical questions, the categorical distinction between social and cognitive evolution remains in place here. There exists quite a lot of, often implicit, evolutionary thought in IR, but many of the more explicit attempts to apply evolutionary theory have not been satisfactory.

We will then present applications of a social evolutionary perspective to the study of world politics/IR broadly understood. Their purpose is not to provide fully-fledged case studies, but rather to demonstrate, in a condensed form, what the analysis of long-term change looks like when seen from the perspective of social evolutionary theory. In fact, making a compact case for the usefulness of such a perspective is the aim of this entire book – longer elaborations of these applications are to be found in (extant or forthcoming) publications by its individual authors.[3]

The first application deals with the evolution of a system of world politics understood in terms of different forms of organizing political authority; the second with reading (violent) conflicts and peacebuilding as evolving contexts; the third with the evolution of diplomacy as a practice and institution. While all these applications can easily be identified as 'core' subjects in the study of world politics both within IR and from various interdisciplinary angles (IR Theory, IR/Peace and Conflict Studies, Diplomatic Theory/History), it is the unique charm of a social evolutionary take on them that it, in fact,

---

3   Although it is necessary to point out that, given the by now almost decade-long history of conversations on the present book, it is not entirely fair to describe it as a condensed amalgamation of previously existing individual contributions; contrariwise, in fact, many of those individual studies benefitted from the conversations in question.

requires no ontological fixation. By being empirically and theoretically open to accommodating the evolution of, most notably, structures, processes and practices, the social evolutionary perspective is broad and inclusive. In this context, it can also be read as an invitation to reflect on how different literatures on, for example, international structures and international practices relate to one another.

A short conclusion summarizes the potential benefit of a social evolutionary perspective for the understanding of world politics in terms of long-term historical change and addresses the challenges that our perspective poses for disciplinary studies on world politics. It is time to rectify what we hold to be a rather parochial reception of social and evolutionary theories on the part of IR, a reception that would be well worth exploring as a process of social evolution in its own right.

2 The coevolution of society and evolutionary theory through four Axial Ages

As part of the longer route mentioned earlier, the following reconstruction of some of the significant stages in the evolution of the theory of evolution also reflects the differentiation between social evolutionary theory and the broader evolution of society. The evolution of evolutionary theory is closely related to major societal transformations. In order to account for both interrelated processes we will be resorting in subsequent sections to the notion of Axial Ages, arguing that fundamental societal transformations in human history, as discussed in Axial Age theory, can be read simultaneously as evolutionary changes in society as well as in the ways that evolution has been theorized in successive eras. In these different eras we also witness the differentiation between cognitive and social evolution and, within the latter, between normative and functional evolution. While we focus here on the European tradition, recourse to Axial Age theory embeds this within a broader Afroeurasian paradigm. Likewise, although the sources we draw from come mainly from the Western tradition, this should not obscure the fact that there exist many similarities in the Eastern traditions (China, Islam), both regarding changes in societal structure and the ways of theorizing societal evolution in each era (see, for example, Jung 2022). The core argument is that social evolutionary theory and social structure coevolve, which also means that looking at the latter is a prerequisite for understanding the former, in particular for understanding theories of evolution *avant la lettre*. Evolutionary theory, so our argument runs here, did not start in modernity but, looking at the core philosophical and political theories of each era, had many predecessors in all but name. Explicit theories of social evolution, though, remain a product of what we propose to call the 'Fourth Axial Age of Global Constitutionalism', starting roughly in the middle of the eighteenth century and shaped by functional differentiation of (world) society.

2.1 Pre-Axial segmentary societies and the First Axial Age: Learning and institutionalizing equality and liberty, ca. 100,000–3500 BCE

The starting point of social evolutionary theory, historically speaking, was the emergence, or evolution, of a consciousness of freedom (Hegel) among the human species and how this affected the way humans in this epoch 'theorized' their social surroundings, in the sense that they drew upon new folk models of it. In that sense, social evolutionary theory began as a 'science of the concrete' in the age of segmentary societies of nomadic hunter-gatherers (100,000–5000 BCE) (Lévi-Strauss 1968: 11–50). Rather than providing (written) theories, this era, which predated the invention of script, saw the invention of myths – as expressed, for example, in cave paintings/rock art or figurines – that can, retrospectively, be read as the evolution of an understanding of the freedom of human action and, therefore, the general possibility of change of social structure. While segmentary societies are often seen as static, the central point here is that this stasis must be seen as a deliberate choice, which only makes sense when viewed against the backdrop of a general human awareness in this era that societies could change (Godelier 1973: 316; Habermas 2020: 178; Hegel 1986: 12; Lèvi-Strauss 1972). Social structures were established that were meant to prevent this change from taking place, in particular the erection of permanent hierarchies of (political) domination. While this was still speculation in the works of Freud and Marcuse, some evidence has been provided in more recent advanced research on chimpanzees as well as in social anthropology research to suggest that the quest for institutionalized hierarchies has accompanied *homo sapiens* forever. Thus, research indicates, insurgencies by male chimps, sometimes by female chimps too, could be followed by egalitarian cooperation among groups of males or females to dominate the rest of the herd, sometimes for a decade or longer. However, the big apes were neither able to institutionalize their advance, nor interested in institutionalizing it and passing it to their offspring. The reason for this discontinuity appears to be the (nearly) total lack of the capacity for an informative, conversational use of language (Boehm 2001: 182, 187; de Waal 1982: 237f, 252f; Jablonka and Lamb 2005: 202; Muller and Mitani 2005: 276; Wilson 2012: 366). Apes learn to a considerable extent instrumentally (strategically), and to some extent emotionally, and they can observe themselves. However, because they have not acquired language and cannot converse, they cannot take an impartial position reciprocally. Therefore, in Habermasian terms, they cannot make impartial truth claims and construct a theory or a societal institution or teach their kids how to maintain the cultural advances made by their parents.

Quite differently, humans – at least since the invention of language – always come into the world already socialized and imitate language from birth onwards as babies do in their first protospeech acts (Greenwood 2015). Whereas chimps learn alone, human learning – cognitive as well as emotional or normative – is from the very beginning social learning, and that is why the evolution of society and personal-cognitive learning must be understood as coevolutionary. Social anthropologists assume that, at the earliest stage of human societies (*homo sapiens sapiens*), alpha males tended to dominate groups of hunter-gatherers, but this early period was soon followed – most likely as a result of the emergence of complex language systems – by a seemingly very long period of widely implemented egalitarian and cooperative societies often, but not always, with flat hierarchies, that remained unstable and limited to special functions (hunting, war) and a rather mild form of patriarchy (Knauft 1991, 1994; Boehm 2001). In other words, egalitarianism was not a precivilizational, almost animal-like precursor of 'real' (viz. hierarchical) society, but a conscious choice by which humans dissociated themselves from hierarchical alternatives. Contemporary social anthropology has quite a lot of evidence that the 'antidomination' normative system of these societies represented a conscious political choice in contradistinction to preceding relations of domination – that is, what we see here is an early form of social evolutionary theory in the sense that the conscious establishment of anti-hierarchical institutions suggests that early humans were aware of social evolution, and tried to prevent change once egalitarian societies had been successfully established (Sigrist 1979: 110–112, 159, 185–200; Graber and Wengrow 2021). This new normative system of the pre-Axial epoch and the First Axial Age was based on a 'reverse dominance hierarchy' (Boehm 1993) and secured by a comprehensive, yet comparatively moderate system of surveillance and punishment (Boehm 1993: 240–254; Woodburn 1982; Knauft 1991; Gardner 1991; Gardner 2014; Cashdan 1980; Almeida 2014). Being rooted in an overarching 'law of equality' (Clastres 1974: 159), segmentary societies thus have an enlightened, explicit and distinct knowledge of the anti-hierarchical structure of their community, an articulated interest in its maintenance and reproduction, and they pass on their knowledge to their children through teaching and moral education in the form of myths (Boehm 2001: 187, 193 f.).

This explains why the myth of liberation is an important part of the science of the concrete. Combined with the sanctioned reverse dominance hierarchy, internalized through socialization, the science of the concrete represents in the Kantian sense the practical and performative side of humanity's evolutionary 'exit from self-inflicted immaturity'. While pre-Axial societies, to the best of our knowledge, developed an objectifying knowledge of the *structure* of their own societies (through language), they had not yet systematically developed an objectifying history of social development. For that we have to turn to the First Axial Age with its lists of kings and Pharaohs, and the Second Axial Age when – in opposition to a rise in hierarchical societal structures – the memory of egalitarianism and a right to liberty became deeply engrained in myths (e.g. that of Ulysses) and religious belief systems (e.g. God's compact with the people of Israel on Mount Sinai). What we, in a revision of Jaspers' original scheme, refer to as the First Axial Age may be dated from around 3500 BCE, when city-states emerged in Egypt and Mesopotamia, and eventually in the Asian subcontinent (the Harappa culture), Africa (Punt, Kush) and today's Syria, to the

Bronze-Age collapse around 1200 BCE. This period saw the emergence of city-states and the world's first state (Egypt from around 3200 BCE) and eventually the first empires, writing and written law, institutionalized factional politics and institutionalized pantheons (Van de Mieroop 2016).

2.2 The Second Axial Age or the age of counter-present theorizing of stratified/imperial class societies and the memory of universalism, ca. 800–200 BCE

Relatively small, nomadic or seminomadic societies with at best flat hierarchies still existed after the differentiation of centre and periphery. Amid the anarchic peripheries of urban-centred, imperial class societies, geographically vast and subject to very little central control, societies now became increasingly exposed to military aggression, annihilation, plundering and enslavement from imperial (city) centres. Early ancient Israel was one of these peripheral societies, already partly agrarian, with a cattle-based economy, as described in the biblical Book of Judges, these judges being the 'big men' of the Hebrew tribes (Ryan 2015; Bohannan 1978).[1] It is easy to imagine that in these societies the memory of a past, transitory age of egalitarianism radicalized into a counternarrative, or, more precisely, a counterpresent memory of an egalitarian past. This happened in the context of the emerging monotheism of the (Second) Axial Age (800–200). Arguably for the first time (Pharaoh Akhenaten's experiment with monotheism only lasted for a couple of decades), the universal equality and dignity of all human beings was systematically and durably interpreted (and stored in written texts; Jaspers 1949, 2021; Assmann 1990, 1995, 2015, 2018; Breuer 1994;).[2]

---

1 The three cities mentioned in Judges are referenced only negatively: alien and unjust, they oppress and exploit the weak, rob and murder strangers, and God is silent.

2 In contrast to Jaspers' 'Eurasia' we use the term 'Afroeurasia' for reasons of very reasonable political correctness, but also because the (imaginary and intellectual) histories of Old Egypt and Old Israel are too closely entangled,

This combination of universalization and storage in texts permitted this counter-present memory to be referred back to throughout the times between the days of Isaiah and those of, say, Rousseau and Marx. The core idea underpinning this counternarrative was to see the present in a non-essentialized way, that is, to theorize about society as open to change, with a normative striving to realize an unprecedented but historically remembered age of 'political and social utopia' (Assmann 2013: 79f; Weinfeld 1987: 242–247, 254f; Uffenheimer 1987: 211, 229).[3] In that way, the biblical story of the Book of Exodus became a kind of paradigm for what can be understood as an evolutionist representation of history as progress, rooted in a consciousness of freedom that is at least prospectively universal and astonishingly modern. That is why Exodus – being part of a larger Afroeurasian tradition of religiously based world images (Eisenstadt 1987: 21) was rightly defined by Assmann as the revolution of the ancient world, deeply embedding a sense of liberty and (possible) evolutionary change – based on the 'poetic memory' of prophetic writers (Buber 2014: 8f.).

The Exodus story sets out a general and novel normative model of universal history, the evolution of emancipation from self-inflicted immaturity. The structurally similar Axial-Age belief systems centring on God (Israel), Nirvana (Buddhism) or ideas (Greece) are different from the particularistic liberation myth of segmentary, egalitarian societies insofar as they are now based on a largely monotheistic structure governed by one universal principle and an overarching notion of a covenant between God (Nirvana, the idea) and each

---

so that one must suppose that Israelian monotheism developed by a (probably reciprocal) process of copy and paste, pick and mix, analyse and recombine from Old-Egyptian religion, which with its strict differentiation of transcendence and immanence belongs to the Axial Age anyway (even if the entire story of Exodus is mere fiction as it probably is). See also Graness's interesting thesis (2017). Again, the monotheism of Akhenaten the rebel Pharaoh (ruled ca. 1353–1336 BCE) is a key point here.

3   All translations in this text are our own. For a sound critique of the basic distinction in modern state theory between stateless barbarism and statist civilization see Eberl 2021.

human, thus inscribing the notion of freedom into this covenant. In that sense the quasi-constitutional covenant turned into a lasting scheme of revolutionary counter-memory based on the notion that under no circumstances must reciprocity, equality and justice be forgotten in the future – and the age-old egalitarian spirit and sense of liberty, as well as means to prevent stasis and unshakable hierarchies, must be remembered. On this basis, revolutions and constitutions can be 'repeated' over and over again.[4] This was already the case in the biblical narrative where, after the suppression of the counter-revolution led by Moses' brother Aron, the covenant was renewed by reference to this scheme, as later on by Paul in early Christianity (see below), by Weitling with respect to the Covenant of the Righteous in 1836 and by Marx, Engels and Wolff in the Covenant of the Communists, all building on the aforementioned scheme. This is not to deny that, in contrast to this scheme (particularly prevalent in Exodus and the Prophets) many religious texts (in Judaism, Christianity, and others) 'have considerable moral ambiguities because of their otherworldliness' (Rorty 1998: 25). More precisely, they justify this-worldly oppression in the name of post-mortem, otherworldly justice. In this respect, the religious and philosophical revolutions of the Second Axial Age suffer from 'unlearning', which happens by repressing the critical power of the counter-memory scheme of egalitarianism and societal transformation by projecting and postponing it to a transcendent future. This, paradoxically, turns the originally subversive counter-present memory of egalitarian structures into an affirmation of the existing, hierarchical world.

In the wider Mediterranean culture of late Antiquity, cognitive and normative learning processes set in that picked up and transformed the counter-present scheme. Between 350 and 450 CE, and after centuries of cultural hegemony in this region of the pagan Greek and Roman political master image (Brown 2002) of city and citizens, the cultural revolutionary fire of an alternative master image was kindled and spread within the entire Roman Empire, mainly by Christian bishops, priests and monks from Asia Minor,

---

4   On the repeatability of the unforgettable event of the revolution see Kant 1977: 361.

the Near East and North Africa, leading to the establishment of the first two Christian states in the Empire's periphery – Armenia and Georgia in 313 and 318 respectively. This was the biblical, egalitarian master image of the poor (*modèle économique*), that contrasted itself with unjust and discriminating city-based class-societies of rich and poor (*modèle urbain*) (Brown 2002: 46, 80; Caner 2021; Duby 1981: 509; Kuhn 1962; Patlagean 1977: 156f.). From this perspective, when pagan Romans looked at 'their society, they saw, above all, cities and citizens, while Jews and Christians had come to see, rather, rich and poor' (Brown 2002: 9). Peter Brown describes the turn from the pagan to the biblical master image as the emergence of a first kind of universal class that the monks formed together with the anonymous poor and that no longer knew any attachment to town and country, but only the universal difference between rich and poor in town and country (Brown 1989: 279; Marx 1972: 390). This was a tremendous cultural revolution. The partisan perspective of the poor that finally prevailed led to a moderate and tolerant Christianization of the Empire (including the adoption of Christianity as state religion by Constantine in 353) not only due to structural causes (economic crises, demographic changes, growing migration, effectiveness of Christian propaganda and networks and the legitimizing potential of Christianity for autocratic rulers; Brown 2002: 8, 10, 47; Garnsey and Humfress 2001: 3; Horden and Purcell 2000: 89–112, 377–383) but also because the *modèle économique* had better arguments on its side than the militarized *modèle urbain*. Thus, the biblical representation of Roman society as the totality of a deeply divided class-society that included an agrarian basic structure described the social reality of Late Antiquity much more appropriately than the *modèle urbain*. Moreover, the New Testament's sentimental longing for an 'unconditional solidarity of open-hearted' individuals unleashed strong emotional powers (Brown 1989: 233–239, 246).[5] Finally, the universalistic concept of justice from both testaments was normatively superior to the exclusive civic master image because it addressed *all* inhabitants of the empire as equals, at least as a normative scheme.

---

5   On the 'pathos of distance', see Nietzsche 1980: 258–260.

2 The coevolution of society and evolutionary theory through four Axial Ages   31

The leading philosopher and one of the most brilliant preachers of this time, St. Augustine (354–430), Bishop of Hippo in North Africa, wrote on that basis in *De Civitate Dei*, the up to then most comprehensive theory of evolution (in all but name). However, Augustine does not reach the cognitive and normative level of modernity of Exodus outlined above, at least as regards the social and political terms he uses, which remain much more hierarchical (bishop, ruler, clerics) than those of their historical antecedent, thereby highlighting the non-linearity of social evolution. However, one strong evolutionary advance in terms of (implicit) theories of evolution is clearly apparent in his writings, namely in his evolutionary theory of performative knowledge and the human subject. Without going into theological detail, Augustine's interpretation of the Holy Trinity and in particular the simultaneity of past (Father), present (the contra-present Son) and future (Holy Spirit, age of solidarity) not only resembles the performative, practical-critical and revolutionary concepts of human will (*voluntas*) by Young Hegelians and pragmatists such as Kierkegaard, Marx and Dewey (Kierkegaard 1941: 162; Kierkegaard 2013: 466; Flasch 2006: 51–53; Habermas 2020: 462–466). It also overcomes the objectifying ontological perspective of philosophical metaphysics favouring tradition (or rather hierarchy) over subjective and 'performatively present experience' (Habermas 2020: 466). In other words, Augustine ascribes to the subject the *possibility* of understanding history in a performative way, as the subject's own *universal* emancipation from self-inflicted immaturity. This emancipation then mirrors the notion of Trinity inner-worldly as the unity of a normatively future-oriented (classless), contra-present (class society) memory (egalitarian past). With this already modern, temporal-historical and performative understanding of the subject, Augustine connects to the older prophetic notion of understanding the expectation of a better future not as prognosis or utopia, but performatively as the result of human interventions (Koch 1995: 256). The change of paradigm from the exclusive and hierarchical master image of the citizen (Rome) to the inclusive and, at least in theory, equality-based master image of the poor can be understood, in evolutionary terms, as an exemplary learning process in relation to the three dimensions of cognitive (sociological) knowledge, normative insight and emotional empathy, striving for a progress in societal solidarity (Brunkhorst 2005).

2.3 The Third Axial Age: Early functional differentiation and the turn to immanence-theorizing societal change, ca. 1000–1750

The turn to immanence during the Second Axial Age which emphasized the possibility of change – understood as a 'human-made' God – made the return to a once existing egalitarian order (largely on a transcendental level) central to social and theological theorizing in the wider Mediterranean cultural realm, and was followed by a second cultural revolutionary turn in monotheism around the year 1000, also referred to as the age of the Papal Revolution. Particularly significant here is the theological interpretation of an immanence of the transcendent, which allowed the Western Church in this period (1075–1122) to anchor key notions of the Second Axial Age in what in retrospect can be understood as the evolutionary shift to modern law, a key foundation of the functional differentiation of society. Somewhat anticipating Hegel's theory of the objective spirit, Roman church intellectuals redefined both Roman and canon law as the incarnation of God, identifying the *Corpus Christi* with the *Corpus Iuris*. In this way law – understood as an instrument of God, in a similar way as in Islam during the same period – became a heavenly-turned-earthly instrument for changing this world for the better (Berman 1991; Brunkhorst 2014). One element of this turn towards immanence was that educated elites and philosophers started to debate around the year 1100 whether (or not – per heretical implication) God exists, making the existence of God dependent on inferential consequences of their own earthly, human reasoning (Berman 1991: 290f; Flasch 1994: 50–61, 94–96). Yet the most important result, in evolutionary terms, of this legal turn to immanence in the Roman church was the invention of modern, professionalized law that was based most fundamentally on a principle of law as universal freedom. In that way universal freedom became the basic category of law, due to a novel mix of Roman civil law (simply a law of coordination and improvement of domination of the ruling classes of empire) and canon law (designed as a law of salvation and emancipation from the misery of this world) (Fried 2007: 172; Köhn 1991; Szabó-Bechstein 1991). This shift to a paradoxical 'law that is freedom' (Luhmann) interlinked with the inner-worldly concept of the 'existence of free will' (Hegel) was the foundation of the Third Axial Age during which the functional differentiation of law took off (Hegel 1976: §29; Luhmann 1981: 62). One side effect, as with many evolutionary changes, was that the impact on societal structures was more profound than contemporaries could have anticipated. Due to the complexity of the new law of universal freedom, a process of legal professionalization immediately set in, aiming in other words to reduce this complexity by structurally coupling law and (legal) science as the first two autonomous functional systems of (early) modern society (Bauer 2018). That was, in other words, the onset of functional differentiation as the prime form of differentiation in (modern) society (not precluding that the occurrence, as in other Axial Ages, of similar developments more or less simultaneously in other world regions, e.g. the Muslim world).

To be sure, the at once normative (law of *freedom*) and functional (*law* of freedom) evolutionary innovation stabilized and augmented the existing strata-based power-structure. Yet, at the same time the political claim to universal freedom and emancipation through law (triggered by legal reforms and revolutions) became a real, imaginable and normatively justifiable possibility, a dynamic largely unknown in the pagan Greek and Roman-dominated cultures of the northern Afroeurasian hemisphere during Antiquity. The Third Axial Age was thus characterized by the somewhat paradoxical interrelationship between a largely unintended functional learning process of societal subsystems, on the one hand, and an intentional cognitive and normative learning process of specific social groups and classes (even the masses of people, as early Protestant movements in the Roman Church realm indicated), on the other. It was the social learning process during Late Antiquity (200–1000 CE) that led to the promotion of the poor from the merely economic category of beggar to the judicial category of plaintiff entitled to appear before the bishop's courts (which were, however, conservative being based on Roman civil law). Even so, the masses were legally and politically perceived as a passive and 'lonely crowd' (Riesman et al. 2020; see also Brown 2002: 69). By contrast, the social learning process affecting the status of the masses in the age of the Papal Revolution activated and organized these masses based on the notion of the *pauperes*. Non-elite groups even started to organize themselves, often with the (by no means disinterested) help of Church elites. This happened, for example, in the Peace and Truce of God Movement, later on in protective associations and local peace militias set up mainly by craftsmen, such as the *Caputiati*, the capuchin men (Köhn 1991; Arnold 2009). The value attributed in this period to labour promoted the status of peasants and other working people (still under the hegemony and rule of clerics and political-military leaders) into a potentially active, self-organized, sometimes social-revolutionary, and sometimes even legislative power. No longer were these masses a 'lonely crowd' as they had been during most of Antiquity (Duby 1981). It was, not least, the significant contribution of the poor in Roman Church realms to the first crusades that fundamentally strengthened the collective agency of the lower social classes. They were no longer mere recipients of plundering, burning and murdering by warriors but became themselves warriors who on their long journeys plundered, burned and murdered first the Jews, then the Arabs, then their Byzantine Christian brethren in Constantinople. They committed these acts – which would today constitute crimes against humanity – in the name of the law and the turn to immanence (of establishing God's kingdom on Earth through human action), as expressed, for example, in the establishment of new states throughout the conquered region (e.g. the Kingdom of Jerusalem), most of them short-lived.

Unintentionally, though, the intolerant and brutal reign of the crusades had a paradoxical effect. The Pope's twelfth-century crusaders disseminated the (written) message of Christian universal freedom, just as modern-day conquerors, from Napoleon to the US and the Soviet Union, spread universal concepts alongside their power-political and military projection, for instance, universal freedom (now based on popular sovereignty) and global constitutional provisions (either democratic or communist, with the US and the Soviet Union both aiming to be champions of anti-imperialism).

Turning back to the Third Axial Age, the lower classes and the Roman church elites of the eleventh and twelfth centuries witnessed a gradual societal transformation. This change in societal structures was based on the underlying 'general concept of freedom', sometimes evolving into 'communal associations with a highly developed political autonomy' of free and equal male individuals (Köhn 1991: 349; Fried 2007). Legal scholars in that period also redefined the doctrine of inheritance in Roman civil law, which basically revolved around the notion that what concerns everyone requires the consent of everyone (*quod omnes similiter tangit, ab omnibus comprebetur*). They then universalized and socialized this doctrine, meant to address only the ruling classes, into a constitutional principle that governed any corporative body and potentially all the people living under it (Berman 1991: 366; Tierney 1982: 21, 24–25; Brundage and Eichbauer 2022). Through this creative reinterpretation of the *quod omnes tangit* principle, even laymen were now able to be represented at general councils of the Roman Church (Tierney 1982: 21). In political theory, these Church Councils were meant to represent the entire People of the Church, including all generations, alive or dead, as a kind of Christian, eschatological popular sovereign (see Möller 2021). Over time, and taking off during the thirteenth century, mendicant orders (like the Franciscans) as well as lay poverty movements mushroomed, the latter organized – as were the many free and republican cities that consolidated in that period too – on the basis of the proto-liberal new law of corporations. This finally culminated in the manifold Protestant uprisings, revolutions and revolutionary wars of the sixteenth and seventeenth centuries. In the course of these complex Protestant revolutions, the idea of the equal freedom of every Christian (legally construed during the Papal revolution) was then combined with the humanistic (secular) concept of self-empowerment of all individuals, whether Christian or not (Cassirer 1994, 2013; Habermas 2020: 724f). While the Papal Revolution thus brought the dualism of transcendence and immanence into the historical (and immanent) realm of an emerging legal sphere, the Protestant Revolution freed immanence almost totally from this dualism by transferring the ultimate decision about the border between immanence and transcendence to the conscience of the individual believer. Transcendence, in other words, no longer affected the social world from the outside, but became part – normatively as well as in terms of social structure (e.g. in Protestant collectives) – of the subjective world of the individual. Starting from there, it hardly comes as a surprise that Zwinglian jurists and intellectuals drew the consequences of this and proclaimed, probably for the first time in modern legal language, universal human rights (see Art. 3 of the Twelve Articles of Memmingen, and comparable later proclamations by English Diggers; Blickle 2003, 2004).

As in many revolutions, not all the potential fruits were harvested. For example, human rights were, if at all, codified in subjective rights of property, but not as political or broader social rights (this has only happened, globally, since the late eighteenth and early nineteenth centuries; Duby 1981, 2020; Flasch 1994: 120). As in the previous epochs discussed here, these evolutionary changes in society also witnessed a transformation of proto-theories of social evolution, that is, the social theories reflecting on how this change came about. One example here would be what can be conceived of as the first functionalist theory of society in that context, written about 1159 by John of Salisbury in his *Politicratus*.[6] However, despite these noteworthy theoretical innovations, the overall impact of the Third Axial Age on the theory of social evolution was relatively meagre. During the sixteenth and seventeenth centuries, social contract theories and political utopias (e.g. Thomas More's) were almost completely decoupled from the hitherto dominant religious salvation-narrative, while an empiricist tradition of (in particular military) historiography that had existed since Greek and Roman times – going back as far as Thucydides – allowed for at least some theorizing on social change as well. However, it was not until the eighteenth century that social contract theories and political utopias

---

6   Again as far as the West is concerned, since, for example, Ibn Khaldun's theory of the state exhibits a similar outlook. John understands society as a progressively rational entity that can improve itself and is oriented towards the monotheistic programme of justice and enabling the rise of individual subjectivities, as a theological, political and legal fight 'against oppression and obstruction' (Duby 2020: 201; see also Szabó-Bechstein 1991: 161f).

were, finally, combined with the newly emerging concept of biological theories of evolution and evolutionist philosophies of history – laying the ground for the emergence of social evolution theories explicitly defining themselves as such.

2.4 The Fourth Axial Age: The planetary age of global constitutionalism and explicit social evolutionary theorizing, ca. 1750–present

Modern social evolutionary theory emerged together with structural changes related to the globalization of core constitutional and legal principles outlined in the previous section, that is, in the context of the mushrooming political-revolutionary and constitutional-reformist changes on a global scale that took place between about 1750 and 1850. The (hierarchical and imperial) outreach of mainly European powers shaped centre–periphery relations between European and non-European world regions reaching out first across the Atlantic (USA, Haiti) and then to other world regions. This decentring of the underlying basic structure of (world) society was, consequently, accompanied by 'the entire immense superstructure' of a major transformation of constitutional theory and in its wake core societal dynamics (Marx 1904: 12). It is important to point out in this context that the dynamic of (global) constitutionalization must not be read as the 'binding together' of functionally differentiated, global systems of politics, that had somehow previously emerged independently of one another, or 'grown apart' from one another. Rather, this process of constitutionalization represented the core of a tight coevolution of the political *and* legal systems of world society, which included the ongoing differentiation that was the condition for their mutual linkage.[7]

As far as the evolution towards global constitutionalization was concerned, the first written and printed constitution of this plane-

---

[7] For an elaborate account in the long historical perspective, see Brunkhorst 2014; for one focused on the modern systems of world politics and global law, see Albert 2002.

tary age was the *constituzione* of Pasquale Paoli in Corsica. Notably, it appeared on the European periphery, not in its powerful heartlands, and was published in the same year as Rousseau's *Discours sur l'origine et les fondements de l'inégalité parmi les hommes* – the latter thus not being the first, but the most advanced and most influential draft of a theory of social evolution at the time (Colley 2021: 17–25). Rousseau was in close contact with leaders in Corsica and even wrote a draft constitution for Paoli, modelled on Swiss cantonal constitutions (Rousseau 2010). The second constitutional draft was the *Nakaz* (the Grand Instruction) of Catherine II of Russia, emphasizing the equality of all men before the law, disapproving of the death penalty and torture. The *Nakaz* was drafted by a commission composed not only of Russians from the propertied classes, but also of non-European, non-Christian people, as well as dispossessed people, women, workers and peasants. It was approved in 1767 and remained in force for four years until it was set aside by Catherine in favour of imperial expansion and the consolidation of her power (Colley 2021: 57–92, 408f). Nevertheless, the *Nakaz* was influential as it made its way not only into French, but also Polish and North American constitutional discourse, especially after Diderot's meeting with Catherine II in 1773 (Butler and Tomsinov 2009).

Both constitutional documents, the Corsican *constituzione* and the Russian *Nakaz*, not only aroused interest throughout Europe and overseas, they ultimately changed the public discourse of European, and increasingly non-European, intellectuals who came to view (global) law as completely immanent by sublating the Protestant dualism God/consciousness. This global (increasingly post-European and post-Christian) Fourth Axial Age of global constitutionalism was therefore characterized by a complete and full worldly-making of transcendence, 'transcendence from within, and transcendence in this world' (Habermas 1991b). This also affected the way in which social change was theorized, and it therefore comes as no surprise that Rousseau's Second Discourse is an empirically grounded (speculative) theory of social evolution that already contains core ideas of the most advanced evolutionary theories of the twentieth century (those of Gould, Lewontin, Kuhn etc.). That is, the fundamental idea of a permanent gradual change through (a) natural selection interspersed with sudden, quickly accelerating periods of revolutionary change (such as punctuational bursts, legal, scientific revolutions etc.), and (b) epigenetic processes (such as allopatric speciation, when populations of the same species become spatially separated). Moreover, anticipating Marx, Dewey and Peirce, Rousseau stressed that all evolution (in human society) contains significant and intentional learning processes that shape humans' imagination and the striving for experimentalism and comparison that forms the normative basis for the central evolutionary role of solidarity and egalitarianism that we witness from the inception of language. This is the social understanding of change that allows us to transcend (if only counter-factually) every existing reality that restricts individual diversity and universality and to strive for social and egalitarian freedom. It is not, however, a linear theory. For one thing, Rousseau makes the 'decisive step into a post-metaphysical thinking' (Geyer 2007: 163, 203) by highlighting that the content of future changes cannot reasonably be foreseen. As Rousseau puts it, 'no philosopher who would be so bold as to say: Here is a limit to which man can reach and which he cannot cross. We do not know what nature allows us to be' (Rousseau 1971: 38; Emerson 1983: 406).[8] Secondly, then, and antedating complex evolution theories that refrain from imagining stability, Rousseau understands the concept of revolutionary change 'no longer as a cyclical upheaval from one stable state to another, but as a permanent, crisis-like structural change that became the guiding historical concept of modernity' (Geyer 2007: 252). Almost 100 years later, in 1848 the *Communist Manifesto* similarly defined revolutionary change as a permanent process: '[t]he bourgeoisie cannot exist without *continually* revolutionizing the instruments of production', that is, the relations of production, that is, all social relations (Marx and Engels 1974: 465). Rousseau's theory of evolution thus, on the one hand, expresses a Hegelian idea of emancipatory

---

8   Iring Fetscher (in a continuation of Cassirer's groundbreaking interpretation from the 1920s) stated in 1960 that Rousseau had thus 'introduced the new idea of the radical structural change of man into the discussion ... in opposition to all the theories of natural law that were available to him.' (Fetscher 1960: 683).

progress (expressed as fundamental freedom), deeply embedded in the social (proto-)theorizing of evolution since the dawn of human civilization. Yet, on the other hand, it suggests that progress does not proceed in a straight line, but rather follows an unpredictable zigzag course in which progression and regression, learning and unlearning are dialectically intertwined.

Novel, revolutionary technologies of dissemination accelerated this process. In the world revolutions and revolutionary world wars during the long turn from the eighteenth to the nineteenth century the spread of the global constitutional 'fever' was underpinned by the rapid development and improvement of ever cheaper media of dissemination: the printing press, (steam) shipping, denser networks of postal services, railroads, photography, intercontinental cables, telegrams, radios, moving pictures, and so on. As Marx and Engels already observed, 'steam-navigation, railways, electric telegraphs' made the 'world market' as well as 'world literature', and 'the unification, for which the citizens of the Middle Ages needed centuries with their miserable highways, the modern proletarians bring about with the railroads in a few years' (Marx and Engels 1974: 471). Constitutional texts and revolutionary manifestos were fed into these communications networks, quickly, at relatively low cost, and in large numbers, thus multiplying and fortifying globalized, interregional and reciprocal interaction (Colley 2021: 136f, 416). From the middle of the eighteenth century, it was not only this constitutional 'fever' that spread, but also the theorizing of these (and other) societal changes, which increasingly took the form of explicit theories of biological and social evolution. In fact, neither of these two sides could claim to have been first. Contrary to the view that biological evolutionary theory was there first, evolutionary theory as a whole in this era developed out of a close interaction and mutual learning between biologists, world travellers and world warriors, travel writers and newspaper men, world revolutionaries, counter-revolutionaries and philosophers and proto social scientists. In that context, the idea of a complete immanence of social evolution – its being triggered by developments in society and not from the outside (God/transcendence, nature, etc.) – took root and simultaneously

2 The coevolution of society and evolutionary theory through four Axial Ages   41

led to the globalization of the underlying notions of solidarity and egalitarianism. In his 1795 paper *On Perpetual Peace*, Immanuel Kant could thus assert that the 'most cruel and devised slavery' on the 'sugar islands' (Haiti that is) is a 'violation of rights in one place on earth' that is 'felt by all' (Kant 1986: 216). However, this generalization of subjective rights into an early notion of human rights is only possible because the globalized world of the time became real not just in theory but in practice. As Kant explains, 'the idea of a world citizen right' is only 'now no longer a fantastic and extravagant conception of law' (ibid.). This is because absolute principles (idea, necessity, human rights, eternal peace) need to be linked to the existence of dissemination media. In Kant's time, global ship and postal traffic made a worldwide spread of knowledge possible. In 1787 it took only a few weeks for the text of the new American Constitution to spread around the world, and for constitutional 'fever' to rise in many places (Colley 2021: 108). Between 1760 and 1775, the number of newspapers doubled, which was very much in line with the great impact of the most productive period of Rousseau's life; and it doubled again between 1775 and 1790, which, in turn, massively amplified the impact of Kant in his most productive period. Kant, like all the enthusiastic partisans of the revolution, was perfectly aware of this and how ideas that might only be read by a small elite might ignite a fire of revolution on a much wider societal scale, because the underlying ideas of freedom, solidarity and egalitarianism resonate and make everyone speak in the vocabulary of the coming revolution of citizens of the world, voicing their claim to 'unrestricted' freedom of speech in order to enable the self-legislation of the public (Israel 2014: 45–48). In the late 1780s, a few years after Kant's essay on Enlightenment, the avantgarde of the Paris Revolution demanded this freedom as the 'first human right' (Israel 2014: 51). Grave violations (from despotism to genocide) continued, but could now be repudiated on the basis of an immanent principle clearly codified and distributed in texts. Such violations could now be communicated globally as contradicting constitutional principles that had been printed and therefore could be read everywhere (Colley 2021: 108). Decolonization from the early nineteenth century would not have been possible on that scale without this evolutionary background condition: the learning of novel ideas and evolutionary change in technologies. The accompanying notion of world citizenship, however imperfectly implemented, thus constituted a 'global public sphere' shaped by 'communicative density and empathy', in which human rights violations could be named as such, communicated, publicized and stigmatized (see our section on global peacebuilding below, Eberl and Niesen 2022: 257, 262). As the speed and density of global shipping and the number of postal stations increased, so did not only the lust for colonial and imperial domination, but arguably even more the width and depth with which human rights' violations and (world) war atrocities were communicated and condemned across the globe (Colley 2021: 112–115, 122–154, 257).

Such a broadly informed and enlightened public – transcending the distinction between alleged centres and peripheries – could not exist in ancient Rome and Greece or during the Third Axial Age because neither the ideational underpinning (complete immanence of equality anchored in the idea of positive law) nor the media of dissemination needed for the rapid cross-regional spread that ensured permanent and structured interrelations had by then evolved (Israel 2014: 35, 50, 54). Central too in this context is the observation that this process was in no way one-sided. The revolution in Haiti was the epitome of a modern global revolution (as only the Eurocentric intellectual discourse in Europe has been slow to recognize); likewise, revolutionary plans and constitutional designs from today's Global South made their way into the West, a dynamic that both Linda Colley and Sujit Sivasundaram highlight and give countless examples of (Colley 2021; Sivasundaram 2020).

It was at the apex of *la Terreur* during the French Revolution that Kant, in 1793, developed the final version of his theory of social evolution as real progression for the better (Kant 1977: 351–368). He argued that, even though it was facing a backlash from revolutionary fervour and counter-revolutionary oppression, the affective moral enthusiasm of revolutionaries and their intellectual supporters working under censorship was a sufficient empirical indicator (a *Geschichtszeichen* as Kant called it with explicit evolutionary undertones) of a 'great event' (viz. punctuational burst) in history, that

2 The coevolution of society and evolutionary theory through four Axial Ages 43

is a real progression of mankind for the better (viz. social learning and cognitive evolution) (Kant 1977: 357–359). Such an event, Kant argues – thereby anticipating the centrality of variation and (negative) selection – 'cannot be forgotten', and therefore can and should be 'repeated' even in the event of its 'failure in misery and cruelty' (Kant 1977: 358, 360f). According to Kant, this 'repetition of ever new attempts' at revolution only ends when a constitution based on truly universal democratic freedom has been consolidated and includes all the people of the world in a cosmopolitan society (Kant 1977: 361f, 365). Kant, in sum, thus constructs the world revolution of 1789 as an evolutionary turning point, a new Axial Age. It is axial because it is not a historical event like many others, but a new reference point in world history 'around which everything revolves and which divides its course into a before and after' (Assmann 2018: 14). Moreover, as in the classical philosophical Axial Age concept of Karl Jaspers, and as entailed in the concept of negative selection, the core point is not the full realization of revolutionary goals, but the fact that these goals have become unforgettable and have hence become part and parcel of the cultural memory of world society to be communicated whenever needed. Furthermore, Kant (like Marx a little later) linked his theory of evolutionary learning to social structures, that is, he combined his evolutionary theory with a theory of the evolution of social structure over different world historical stages often driven by violent contestations and countercontestations (i.e., from segmentary societies to capitalist/popular sovereignty societies).

By drawing on Rousseau's idea of constitutional self-legislation, Kant also rephrased the concept of the autonomy of the subject as the core principle of every philosophical discourse. He thereby took up the thread of performative knowledge, which had hardly developed any further since St. Augustine, and provided an evolutionary theory of subjective reason, grounded in the reflexive and practical, and therefore performative, relation of the subject to itself. In other words, Kant developed an evolution-based theory of (a) intersubjectively binding practical reason (morality), understood as the exit from self-incurred immaturity and combined this with (b) an evolutionary social theory of constitutional change based on the real moral and legal progress of mankind. Subsequent philosophical theories of evolution built on that. Schelling gave this theory of the autonomous subject a more materialist flavour, anticipating the praxis-philosophical turn to the existential and historical materialism of Young Hegelian and American pragmatists – and arguably also underpinning Adler's (2019) theory of cognitive evolution. Kant's concept of the autonomy of the subject as the driving force (and destiny) of social evolution has remained central to social evolutionary theory ever since, which, during the twentieth century, turned into communication-based evolutionary theory.

The first core characteristic in that regard is a growing functionalist focus on the autonomy of systems as evolving social structures. This began, at the level of theories of society, with Marx's focus on the functional autonomy of the economic system of world society, was followed by Durkheim's organic solidarity – a solidarity that must not be mistaken for unity but thought of as a bracket linking and integrating the fundamental functional diversity of society – led to Weber and his focus on divergent and contradictory value spheres, ending up, via Parsons and organizational theory, in complex models of differentiated communication and Luhmann's notion of system autonomy. On the level of theories of cognitive evolution and learning it was most clearly reflected in the post-structural turn to subject autonomy (subjectivation) leading from Rousseau's and Kant's idea of the self-reflexive autonomy of the subject, via Nietzsche, Mead and Heidegger, to the contemporary reconstruction of subject-autonomy, self-determination and self-consciousness in the Foucauldian post-structuralist notion of the discursive empowerment of subject-autonomy. It was also, finally, apparent in the rise of critical theories tracking societal emancipatory autonomy, which proceeded from Kant, Schelling, Hegel and Marx, via Weber, Durkheim, Peirce, Gadamer and Adorno to Bühler and Habermas's theory of societal emancipatory autonomy.

This evolution of evolution theories, which now resort, increasingly explicitly, to the concept of 'evolution', runs in parallel to societal transformations that we have already highlighted, first and foremost the globalization of constitutions and the reflection of this process in evolutionary theory. Note that Kant's concept of subject autonomy was preceded by, and enabled in interaction with, a global practical turn to constitutional revolutions (USA, France, Haiti, rest of the world) and permanent global interaction (visible, e.g., in the emergence of global cities such as London in the early nineteenth century that developed as the hubs of intellectual reflection on social evolution at the time). This Fourth Axial Age of global constitutionalism was thus accompanied by an emergent world society of global communication. To be sure, the progress of dissemination technologies in that period also enabled an unprecedented evolution of destructive forces: hybrid warfare combining land and sea operations and wars becoming *world* wars penetrating (almost) all zones of the globe and producing huge numbers of military and civilian casualties. The arms trade and terror flourished too on global scales. In sum, wars triggered revolutions and revolutions triggered wars, and in both cases there were progressive and retrograde variants, and sometimes one turned into the other, as when liberation movements quickly became despotic (Colley 2021: 25–41, 79f, 115–154, 161–168, 245, 270, 289–295, 304, 321–324, 387, 415–424; Osterhammel 2010). Again, this was a global affair far from having the West necessarily as its centre. The first universal female suffrage was introduced in the Democratic Republic of Pitcairn, a small island in the middle of the Pacific Ocean. This republic lasted from 1838 until 1930 and attracted some Europeans who cherished the citizen rights established there (Colley 2021: 253–260). All this was actually well known to contemporaries, but nationalism and imperialism have almost eradicated it from memory.

The ideas of (egalitarian, solidarist) self-legislation and self-representation have evolved since the second half of the eighteenth century in theory and practice. They permeate philosophical, juridical and political discourses, and affect (world) society's power–knowledge complexes. The process is contradictory (ultimately about positive and negative selections). From a structural perspective, and contrary to many realist and post-colonial theories, this evolution is not only, and even not primarily, about power, self-preservation, colonialism and imperialism. It always did include, and normatively privilege, the seductive, disturbing, disruptive power of disseminated constitutional texts and their commentaries that highlighted equality and justice, allowing, even under the harshest circumstances, despotism, colonial rule, slavery, exploitation, autocracy and other institutions of exclusion to be discursively challenged. Where there is power, there is resistance, and this resistance in evolutionary terms is enabled and normatively supported by the axial changes highlighted above, while leaving space for different cultural expressions of generalized and universalized principles in processes of decolonization (Colley 2021: 357–424). This is what Thomas Jefferson meant by putting faith in the repeatability of constitutional revolutions and linking this to the possibility of comprehensive progress: 'Tho' written constitutions may be violated in moments of passion and delusion, yet they furnish a text to which those who are watchful may again rally and recall the people' (Thomas Jefferson; quoted from Colley 2021: 342f) – somewhat ironically, since this was meant to get rid of slaveholders (of whom Jefferson himself was one).

After Kant's blueprint for a cosmopolitan constitution it became ever more evident that the 'unity of a society encompassing all functions' can only be conceived of at world societal levels (Luhmann 1975: 51–71).[9] The idea of a national collective consciousness proved to be as illusory as the idea of a future unity in the collective consciousness of the proletariat. With globally 'prevailing functional differentiation' and – in addition, transcending Luhmann – with growing democratization based on normative learning underpinning the idea of universal freedom (human rights and the idea of full inclusion being the normative underpinning of functional differentiation), the notion of society itself has been globalized.

That is why it is no surprise that the insight that the nation-state is not the solution but the problem as far as world society is

---

9   In 1912 an observer quoted by Luhmann could only state: 'For the first time all five continents serve as the theatre at the same time' (Luhmann 1975: 53). Even then it was realized that 'worldwide interaction is possible if and when partners can be chosen among all human beings ... without boundaries of society preventing it. An Argentinian might marry an Abyssinian, a Zeelander take a loan in New Zealand ..., a Russian trusts technical constructions tested in Japan, a French writer seek homosexual relations in Egypt, a Berliner sunbathe in the Bahamas' (Luhmann 1975: 53).

2 The coevolution of society and evolutionary theory through four Axial Ages 47

concerned had already emerged during the early nineteenth century, with certain people seeing a solution on the international level (which is what would later emerge as the home turf of IR). Kant wrote his essay on a future League of Nations in 1795. Towards the end of the Philosophy of Right, Hegel resorts to the misty notion of world history, placing all hope in an impersonal world judgment by the world spirit, which his student Marx then transforms, still linking it to the concept of objective spirit, into the evolution of world society read as a history of class struggles. What, however, unites all these theories of society is their assertion that (world) society can no longer be produced by establishing egalitarian relations of freedom within regional boundaries; it can only be fully achieved within a truly global context (Hegel 1976; Marx and Engels 2010). From the observation of this reality of world society Marx drew an important conclusion for the theory of social evolution, namely that, at least since the (in our terminology, not Marx's) Fourth Axial Age, the only science is the science of history (understood as world history). This is why everything social is evolution, while the theory of evolution can only, as Marx wrote – even before the appearance of Darwin's groundbreaking work – explain retrospectively. Feudalism can only be seen (in evolutionary terms) from the perspective of bourgeois capitalist society – but not vice versa (Marx 1967; Marx and Engels 2010). Two courses of action stand out: either to trust in the accidental course of evolution and to adapt normative expectations to this (Luhmann), or to actively engage through 'living forward' (Kierkegaard) or being critically-practical and practically-revolutionary, which is what the American, progressivist pragmatist tradition from Dewey to Rorty takes from the theory of evolution as it consolidated in the Fourth Axial Age (Rorty 1998).

Since the Second World War, and much studied by mainstream IR and international law scholarship, global constitutional integration and (rudimentary) global political integration in international organizations and bureaucracies has taken off (a process that started in the nineteenth century – the Congress of Vienna being often mentioned as the inaugural moment). A democratically organized and participatory inclusive world society is far off. Yet, the idea and often the practice of the political, cultural, social and legal inclusion of everybody (full inclusion in Luhmannian terminology), regardless of social, gender, national, religious, ethnic, sexual and 'racial' background, permeates international public law and 'world public opinion', and shapes the self-understanding of 'international public authority' (Thornhill 2020; von Bogdandy et al. 2017: 115–145; von Bogdandy 2022).[10] Moreover, relations between states can hardly be seen as rooted in mere coexistence but contain strong elements of being bound by law that supports the peaceful co-operation of political units (notwithstanding constant breaches of that principle by the West and non-West; Fassbender 2009).

The post–World War II era saw a consolidation of the idea of global constitutionalism, and the sociology of universal communication (paradigmatically in the three dimensions of autonomy: Luhmann, Foucault, Habermas) is its product and part and parcel of it, in a way its active and activating superstructure. The latter is both reflected and shaped by the communicative turn of subject autonomy which, in Foucault's case, was due to the indistinguishable discursive entwinement of power and knowledge with respect to the autonomy of the subject, whereas Luhmann and Habermas both assume that system autonomy as well as societal emancipatory autonomy can both differentiate reflexively between power and knowledge as well as between validity and facticity. Luhmann and Habermas carry out the communicative turn in sociology almost simultaneously (although independently of each other and on the basis of different motives). Habermas spells it out normatively, Luhmann cognitively (Apel 2011: 92–137, 2016).

---

10 Full inclusion is already articulated in the *Charter* that prescribes 'promoting and encouraging respect for human rights and for fundamental freedoms for all without distinction as to race, sex, language, or religion' (Art. 1 [3] UN; Art. 76 UN), and to 'promote: a. higher standards of living, full employment, and conditions of economic and social progress and development; b. solutions of international economic, social, health, and related problems; and international cultural and educational cooperation'(Art. 55 UN).

3 Contemporary social evolution and social evolutionary theories

3.1 Social evolution and theories of society

As demonstrated in the previous section, evolution is firmly ensconced in modern social theory, and particularly in what could be termed 'comprehensive' social theories that seek to provide accounts of the entirety of the social world. In fact, no serious comprehensive social theory does not share the view that, in one way or another, 'society is the outcome of evolution' (Luhmann 2012: 251). This is why 'since Marx, Spencer and Durkheim, the theory of society has been a theory of social evolution' (Brunkhorst 2014: 1), a dynamic that became even more explicit with twentieth-century social theorists such as Luhmann, Elias and Habermas. But there are also less obvious candidates, and here we draw on Foucault's post-Darwinian rejection of Lamarckian evolutionism and its replacement with a non-linear analysis of society that highlights the 'hierarchical complexity' (Commons and Ross 2008) of genealogical layers that engender society's discursive fundamentals – in other words, the evolution of 'regimes of truth' and '*épistèmes*'. We suggest that there is a broad overlap and a (dialectical) complementarity not only with regard to systems theory, critical theory and poststructuralism, but also – and this is specific to social sciences such as IR – between evolutionary theory, genealogy, and social/interregional/global history, which cannot be completely separated from each other for both substantive and heuristic reasons.[1] While the social evolutionary components in Luhmann's work are obvious from the outset and his *Theory of Society* (2012) devotes an entire section to social evolutionary theory, orthodox perspectives on Habermas and Foucault tend to underestimate the degree to which evolutionary thinking shaped their work. Based on a burgeoning literature that moves beyond this, and from which we draw, we suggest that a thorough engagement with Foucault and Habermas brings to the fore not only strong influences from social evolutionary theory, but also reveals a range of complementarities with Luhmann. Without aiming to artificially merge these otherwise quite diverse theories, we suggest that a conjoined reading is warranted. It would enable us to draw on a growing literature that highlights epistemological and ontological overlaps between them (Kneer 1996; Stäheli 2000; Åkerstrøm Andersen 2003; Borch 2005), thereby challenging those – in our view outdated – perspectives that tend to replicate arguments about an alleged fundamental incommensurability.

Habermas's œuvre in particular, beginning with his Ph.D. thesis (Habermas 1954), is closely related to evolutionary theory. In his early work Habermas developed a strictly post-metaphysical and anti-teleological philosophy of history (Habermas 1963), which was closely related to the evolutionary theory of the 1950s. One of the basic ideas was that theory and its practical and critical intentions, as well as its epistemic implications, are part of the same evolutionary processes that the theory analyses (Habermas 1968). After the linguistic turn, Habermas combined the ontogenesis of cognitive and moral competencies with a functional theory of evolutionary adaptation (Habermas 1976, 1981a, 2004). Finally, he also constructed his theory of law on the evolution of the functionally differentiated system of positive law (Habermas 1992; Luhmann 2004). Moreover, overcoming the animosities between Habermasian and Luhmannian camps that existed in the past, more recent literature highlights a number of epistemological and structural similarities between these two

---

1   A very good example for such 'complementarity work' would be Chris Thornhill's new sociology of (international and global) constitutions (see, for example, Thornhill 2014, 2020, 2021).

approaches, including the recourse both have to the notion of social evolution. The linguistic turn made visible the centrality of language and communication that has driven human evolution ever since the central role of chatting during the pre-Axial Age. Thus, on the methodological level, a new approach to critical systems theory is evolving that is a Habermas-Luhmann hybrid, in particular with respect to legal theory (Amstutz and Fischer-Lescano 2013; Möller and Siri 2016; Schecter 2019). From a critical point of view, the driving force of social evolution is an operation called negation (disagreement) – this is a theme central to Young Hegelians and critical theory as well as to systems theory and post-structuralism, thereby linking Foucault, Habermas and Luhmann. It also features strongly in our approach (see below). The accumulation of negations triggers algorithmic evolution (i.e. variation, selection, restabilization) as well as cognitive and normative learning processes. In one major variant, this echoes our focus below on communications as the central mechanism of evolution, where 'the Marxist dialectic of productive forces and relations of production is replaced by a dialectics of egalitarian [emancipatory] and repressive communication' (Möller 2021). In his *Critical Theory of Legal Revolutions: Evolutionary Perspectives*, Hauke Brunkhorst (2014) understands the evolution of law as the result of normatively motivated legal revolutions. Revolutions here are conceived as a kind of punctuational burst (Gould and Lewontin 1979). However, they do not appear out of nothing. They only occur within state-building in stratified class-societies (from 3500 BCE onward) and in functionally differentiated class-societies (from 1000 CE onward), and they do so under two conditions: (a) the existence of long-term cognitive, social and moral learning processes, due to religious rationalization, highly contested philosophical and religious discourses, structural conflicts and class-struggles; (b) the existence of a technically advanced legal order especially for the coordination of the material interests of imperial ruling classes. The learning process terminates in the cognitive and normative insight that social structure is not a natural destiny but can be changed through emancipatory or repressive political action.[2] Under the 'favourable' conditions of a serious crisis of legitimization of established orders, this combination of normative learning and preadaptive functional advances culminates in legal revolutions. Their achievement is the constructive invention and reinvention of a growing and ever more egalitarian, functionally differentiated legal system – later defined normatively as 'law that is freedom' (Kant), and defined functionally as the 'immune system' of society (Luhmann 1995, 2004). The new, revolutionary modern law, including international law, reflects the insight that the structure of human societies can be changed by the 'practical-critical activity' of cooperating actors (Koskenniemi 2001). However, modern law is tricky, paradoxical (Luhmann, Derrida, Teubner) and dialectical (Marx, Adorno, Habermas). It enables an enduring emancipatory praxis and stabilizes progressive advances (see also Kratochwil 2019), yet it also undergirds unprecedented formations of class-rule and international hierarchies, as well as (class-, gender- or race-based) oppression and exploitation. Therefore, with the emergence of modern society, law became a kind of pacemaker for social evolution (Luhmann 2004), for better or worse, and with no teleology that goes beyond the fragile plans and expectations of social actors and agencies, and other 'epigenetic' constructions (Möller 2021).

As far as Foucault is concerned, it would seem too simplistic to conclude that his was not an evolutionary theory from the fact that 'evolution' is not listed in the index of his collected works (see Foucault 1994: 867). Thus, his genealogical method is directly focused on the triad variation, selection and restabilization. In Foucauldian terms, one begins the investigation by identifying a given discourse (or episteme, or dispositive, Foucault conceived of the selective

---

2 As discussed extensively in the previous chapter, we agree with a recent turn in anthropology that suggests that there is every reason to assume that pre-civilization (a.k.a. hunter-gatherer) societies were as much based on experiments with social structure, cognitive learning and a sense of the contingency (and therefore the possibility of change) in social order as the script-based societies with which this is usually associated. We leave open the question about traces of proto-social-evolution theorizing in such societies, focusing in this book on modern social evolutionary theory.

element in different ways throughout his career), only then to jump back to a point before that discourse stabilized, in order to capture its beginning that caused a discursive break (variation), which caused the new discourse and its effects to prevail (restabilization). Given the unconventionality of claiming Foucault as an evolutionary thinker, all these three steps need to be unpacked with a view to highlighting their evolutionary character.

Firstly, stabilization. The entire and consistent thrust behind Foucault's œuvre was an attack on approaches to social analysis that highlighted stability and invariance. Attacks on functionalism and positivism are cases in point, but the basis of his work was an attack on structuralism. The structures that gave structuralism its name, whether linguistic, mythical or, more specifically, embodied in social forms, were famously posited as ahistorical. In the mature formulation of Lévi-Strauss, the job of the analyst was to identify, analyse and compare what he called manifest or observable structures, for example, cooking and gendered division of labour, in order to identify the underlying latent and unobservable structure (Lévi-Strauss ([1953] 1993). Foucault and others who came to be known as post-structural thinkers earned that moniker simply by asking 'What if there are no latent structures?' This is an evolutionary question: it highlights how things do not stand still, but are forever changing, which means that we have to turn away from explaining stability, which is an ephemeral phenomenon, towards studying variation.

Secondly, variation. Manifest structures, ephemeral as they may be, are socially real, which means that there is a social mechanism of some kind that holds them in place. If this is not a latent structure, then what is it? It was to answer this question that Foucault introduced first the term 'episteme', then 'discourse', and then 'dispositive'. The idea was to come up with a conceptualization of the social that was not entirely static, but did explain how so much social energy goes into keeping things as they are. Discourses stay the same largely due to the power/knowledge nexus. Power is productive of social life and is usually a stabilizing force. However, it is also inherent in the social that relations between humans and things change, which means that things that were not problematic before (e.g. a certain form of hierarchy, a certain form of violence), now become so.

New questions spell new variation in the discourse, which, if the invariance-breaking force is strong enough, spells change. Foucault's best-known works detail how this happened, dealing first with how we think about atypical mental states and then with sexuality.

Thirdly, restabilization. Foucault consistently underlined how restabilization should be thought of not primarily in moral terms, as emancipation, but in analytical terms, as how specific practices are inscribed in the social, as well as in each individual, by specific forms of power (as a contest of wills, as discipline, as governmentality; Neumann and Sending 2010). The *locus classicus* is the opening pages of his *Discipline and Punish* (Foucault [1975] 2020), where a description of a man being tortured during one century gives way to a description of how inmates are disciplined in the following century. The obvious thrust of both practices is to restabilize the discourses of power of which they are constitutive parts, with one discourse (of surveillance) having evolved to take the place of another (of punishment).

The theoretical similarities between Foucault and Luhmann (see Stäheli 2000) have been highlighted and built upon especially by the Luhmannian Copenhagen School (the *locus classicus* being Åkerstrøm Andersen 2003), but also feature strongly in works that highlight the similarities between the Foucauldian and Luhmannian conceptions of power and the role of power in shaping (the evolution of) society (Stäheli 2000; Borch 2005).

These diverse bodies of theory from Foucault, Habermas and Luhmann seem to be converging around two paradigmatic pillars: first, a constructivist logic that highlights the centrality of a sequencing of communications (or discourse) as the central mechanism of social evolution; second, an interest in the systemic effects of social evolution on society, with a particular focus on complexity. The formal sequencing of communications challenges an analogy that equates natural with social evolution. If one were to apply such an analogy, what evolved in society as its basic units, and what triggered evolution, would be actors (for example humans, states, non-state organizations, or other units, such as civilizations).³ Consequently, such approaches employ an analogy between actors in the social world and what Dawkins (1976) calls 'selfish genes' in the natural world. In such a perspective, actors are regarded as the 'masters' of social evolution. In our view, this dramatically overestimates the ability of humans, states or other actors to control causes and effects in social evolution. And it dramatically ignores the fact that the very actorhood of these units, as Meyer and Jepperson (2000) explain, is itself a social construction, that is, a contingent outcome of social evolution rather than its origin. Enquiring about society's basic units – or those of world politics such as states – thus requires, in the first place, challenging views of actorhood prevalent in the fundamental equating of genes and actors. Serious social theory is urgently needed precisely for that purpose when talking about *social* evolution.

Against this background it is not surprising that those theories of social evolution that are not mere transpositions of theories of natural evolution have recourse to a constructivist logic, because the constructivist framework addresses 'communication all the way down' (Albert et al. 2008; Luhmann 1995). This basic assumption is shared by Foucault, Habermas and Luhmann. It suggests that society's basic unit, and in fact the foundation of all social order, is communication – or, in the case of Foucault, discourse as the condition of communication. As in Habermas, since the Second Axial Age – that is, since the emergence of politically centred imperial class societies based on agriculture and handwritten papers – we can trace in written sources and elsewhere that discourses are the ever-fluid source of variation and the spontaneous production of contingent power–knowledge complexes. The key question to ask from the perspective of a theory of evolution, then, is how specific communications (and discourses) emerge, stabilize or disappear. What is of key interest are not single instances of communication (a

---

3   Note that there are theoretical biologists who study human societies without drawing on such an analogy; evolutionary transition scholars (e.g. Maynard Smith and Szathmány 1995; Bouchard and Huneman 2013) would be a case in point. See also Wendt 1999: 321.

word uttered, a sigh, a rolling eye), but the clustering of communications into complex social forms as 'carriers' of social evolution, such as discourses, practices, memes, institutions, norms, semantics, structures and forms of actorhood.[4] Societal order is, therefore, not only 'the outcome of evolution' (Luhmann 2012: 251), it is, at the same time, evolution's always pre-existing boundary condition. It is the permanent 'cultural evolution of pronounceable memes, words, leading the way' (Dennett 2017: 220). This is why we always speak of *re*stabilization instead of mere 'stabilization' (Luhmann 2012). A constructivist logic of social evolution traces how order as an emergent and contingent phenomenon evolves on the basis of countless interconnected communications. In other words, structures are communications. On the one hand, this requires us to ask how communications cluster into family 'tree[s] of derivation of a discourse' (Foucault 1972: 147) that generate forms of societal differentiation and normative constraints. On the other hand, the question is how structures emerge not only out of shared understandings of reality but also out of contestations. This position seems to be backed strongly by the epigenetic turn in biological evolutionary theory that became ever more prominent during the last decade (Jablonka and Lamb 2010, 2014: 373–424; Carey 2012; Moore 2015; Rosenfield and Ziff 2018).

This fundamentally constructivist analysis of 'society as communication', with an endless sequence of communications creating, changing and often being their own boundary conditions of possibility, defies a view of the social world in terms of an ontological distinction between separate 'levels'. Whenever such levels are distinguished – one might think here of the distinction between micro and macro levels, between agency and structure (Wendt 1999)

---

4   The concept of memes can be found in Daniel C. Dennett's theory of cultural evolution. As Dennett (2017: 176) notes, what he terms 'cultural evolution' is different from natural evolution in that what evolves are not genes or actors perceived as species but, to play on Dawkins, 'selfish words' (Dennett 2017: 189) that 'evolve by differential replication' and 'cluster in larger meme complexes'; these meme complexes can be conceived as 'the least unit of sociocultural information' (Wilkins 2008: 1647).

or between international and domestic systems – they should be viewed not as ontological distinctions but as operative markers of communication, that nevertheless allow analytical references to be made to empirical instances where they are treated (e.g. by political actors or IR scholars) as substantive levels. In that capacity they can serve as a useful bridge between communication-based approaches that link them with, for example, the distinction between interaction, organization and society (Luhmann 1995), or materiality-based approaches highlighting the 'nexus' of situations (Hirschauer 2014).

Having situated our study in relation to a broader paradigmatic tradition that builds on modern social theory but has deep roots in proto-social evolutionary thinking across the ages (see Chapter 2 above), we will now elaborate in greater detail on the role of communication in accounting for the formal logic of social evolution. Drawing on Luhmann (2012) we focus on the sequencing of communication as a threefold (discursive and cognitive) process involving the variation, selection and restabilization of single communication 'units' that cluster in discourses and (as in Dennett 2017) meme complexes. This also relates to the structural coupling of social evolution with cognitive evolution, again highlighting overlaps between Luhmann and Habermas, especially regarding the starting point of negation mentioned above. As Luhmann (1997: 461; see Wimmer 1996: 115) explains, 'all variation ... is contradiction as disagreement, hence, not in the logical meaning of contradiction but in the originally dialogical meaning'. Similarly, Habermas (1981b: 445–52) states that 'dialectic is resistance in relations of domination [..., that] *is* saying no'. That is why we find social evolution in human, communication-societies, as societies of 'dialogical encounters' (Graeber and Wengrow 2021: 47) out of which, for example, social experiments like building cities originally emerged.

The objective and hence (at least as a whole) uncontrollable process of social variation, selection and restabilization is always already accompanied by a process of permanent cognitive rationalization and rational learning among social groups and communities of practice, trying to increase their capacity to control and stabilize their worldviews and determine their life, as well as their private, public and political autonomy. This learning – and we agree here with Emanuel Adler (2019) – can be seen as normative evolution, defined as the structural coupling between human consciousness and (communication-based) social systems.[5] This also figures in Elias's (1976) and Linklater's (2016) accounts of increasing civilization, understood as the regulation of the articulation of affections through social institutions, in particular through monopolizing violence. Evolutionary learning is the result of internal cognitive reasoning and the emergence of new ideas and, if successful, leads to the establishment of new 'normative constraints' (Brunkhorst 2014) which do not steer the evolution towards a final destination (*telos*) but commit the social actors and agencies for some (unforeseeable) time to a certain evolutionary direction with a certain variety of included and excluded possibilities of variation and selection (change). Such learning processes often consist in overcoming the paradigmatic blindness of a certain master image. As the eminent historian Peter Brown has shown, and as we have highlighted above, throughout the Roman Empire the master image of the city and the citizen blanked out the relevance and even the existence of the majority of non-citizens, living either in the city as a huge and ever-changing number of migrants or in the rural environment and making up the vast majority of the Roman population. However, after the fourth and fifth centuries CE the intensified Near Eastern discourse of Jews and Christians on the biblical image of the poor challenged, and finally replaced, the classical master-image of cities and citizens. The learning consisted in overcoming the cognitive and normative blindness of the classical master image because Christian bishops in particular conceived the naked poor literally: as universal figures but stripped of all wealth once confronted with God's judgment. Therefore, the new master image for the first time cognitively covered the totality of Eastern Roman imperial society and its entire population (except the slaves). Moreover, it no longer represented the poor in *normative terms* as passive beggars, but for the first time as the active plaintiffs accusing the rich and the structure of the entire class society – factually including the major side-effect of the rise of

---

5   On the structural coupling of politics and other systems see Luhmann 2000: 372–74.

the bishops to imperial power (Brown 2002). Thus, such learning by societies can be described as real cognitive and normative progress of knowledge in Habermas's sense (from particular to total, from affirmation to critique of class structure) and as a real change in the power structure through a power-knowledge discourse in Foucault's sense. Moreover, while the new master image includes preadaptive advances in mass action (from beggar to plaintiff) that later can be used for revolutionary change – as during the great (papal) legal revolution or the English, French, Haitian and American political revolutions – or for a further *restabilization* of class-rule etc. (often as the outcome of 'failed' revolutions).

With a view to variation, then, social evolutionary theory is primarily – in addition to learning and the emergence of creative innovations – about the importance of contestations or 'negation' (Luhmann 1995: 357–404; Brunkhorst 2014). This is the fundamental *social* underpinning of change. More precisely, it is about the always existing possibility of contestation of communications in human society, understood as the communication of a 'no' (Stetter 2014). It also is about new communicative ideas that challenge entrenched ways of doing things. A 'no' – which can also be a creative and apparently novel way of doing things and therefore does not necessarily need to be a contestation of the confrontational type (i.e. clearly communicating such a 'no') – marks a disturbance of entrenched societal practices. Contestations thus understood go directly to the heart of the main problem that social evolution has to overcome in order to generate societal complexity and trigger evolution, namely how to deal with so-called double contingency in communication (Luhmann 1995: 103). Double contingency entails the impossibility of generating shared meaning, in the sense of complete mutual understanding. Social communication always has to mediate the problem of the inaccessibility of other people's minds and the impossibility of deciphering their 'real' intentions. Even in a social system with only two participants, how information is understood is contingent for both of them (hence 'double' contingency). Dealing with double contingency thus regularly leads to institutionalized forms of rendering the often unlikely acceptance of communication offers more likely – privileging the 'yes' on the basis of tradition, norms, shared life-worlds or media of communication (such as power, money and law) – for otherwise a temporary fixation of social structures would be impossible, entailing the unpredictability of *any* social arrangement and thus impairing individuals' need to make sense of the world (Luhmann 2012: 190–99). If the likelihood of communicative negations (or innovations) and therefore of variations in society is kept at bay, for example by tradition, and if the spatial spread of communications is contained reducing cross-polity contacts across large distances and cultures, social evolution can be expected to proceed at a slower pace. The Neolithic revolution was not a watershed from that perspective. Even before that, hunter-gatherer societies maintained long-distance contacts and trans-societal institutions, thereby establishing webs of communications sustained by annual meetings, rituals and gift-giving – outbreeding too was a necessity in tribes that usually comprised only 20–200 people (reflected from an IR perspective in Buzan and Little 2000: 115–33). The allegedly incremental nature of change in hunter-gatherer bands (from our point of view, more of a conscious cognitive strategy to disenable stratification and permanent domination by a specific ruling class) is attributed also in IR literatures to a seemingly consensus-oriented and egalitarian set-up in segmentary human societies prior to the emergence of the first major cities around 3500 BCE, which saw the institutionalization of hierarchies and a mushrooming of contestations (primarily between leaders), as well as the restabilization of these contestations in the form of conflicts and new social structures, such as war, which can be read as the onset of an 'offensive realism world' (Tang 2013: 43; Buzan and Little 2000). Recent research in anthropology questions this romantic view of pre-Neolithic societies, and there is growing evidence that these societies were diverse internally and in relation to each other and experimented with many social forms, including hierarchies and inequalities. However, the emergence of script certainly made a change for it allowed novel forms of voicing communicative negations, for example during absence, while in the modern era other technological innovations such as the printing press, the telegraph and the internet continue that trend. Any widened pool of variations that can be uttered and experimented with goes hand in hand with an increasing likelihood of contestations, for example in relation to challenging the political status quo (Luhmann 2000). That modern society observes itself as ever-changing further accelerates such dynamics, for it legitimizes changes to the status quo based, for example, on notions of 'progress' or, as Foucault highlights, due to the relative legitimacy 'resistance' enjoys in the context of modern (global) governmentality (Merlingen 2003; Jaeger 2014; Buzan and Lawson 2015). To be sure, similar dynamics can be discerned in earlier epochs too, as, for example, in the long history of nomad resistance until early modernity (Beckman 1999; Khazanov and Wink 2001). Throughout human history, new media of communication – such as language, scripture, the printing press, the telegraph, the internet, etc. – have undergirded the pools of variation in societal communications based on innovation or contestation. This has also intensified the pressure for a reduction of complexity, for example by establishing social institutions that challenge communications in a way that renders their acceptance more likely, but, as Habermas (1976) shows in his work, also underpins social evolution in terms of socio-cognitive learning, rational problem-solving, and rationalization as far as cognitive evolution is concerned (Weber 1978; the latter is known as 'creative variation' in Adler's terms; Adler 2019: 219).

Selections in social evolution can then be understood as a broader communicative project, which ensures that variations are not forgotten, in particular if they have triggered learning processes. Selection thus means that specific variations are picked up and remembered in future communications. In terms of a theory of evolution, selections can be understood as preadaptive advances that might (or might not) consolidate in new forms of social order. They are not yet about 'sorting' (Vrba and Gould 1986), the restabilization of contestations that condense into expectations about (legitimate) new structures and new societal orders. They are about making alternatives available in future communications and discourses. In other words, selections in social evolution relate to often irreversible, revolutionary changes in the discursive logic in both social struggles and more cooperative settings, such as within communities of practice. The new variations may be accepted or rejected, that is, referred to as positive or negative selections in evolutionary theory. However, they can no longer be forgotten (as Kant had already noted with respect to the variations triggered by the French Revolution; Kant 1977: 361). In some cases, preadaptive advances function as a kind of counter-memory, such as when the memory of the fictive Exodus story of the Revolution of the Old World (Mediterranean/Middle Eastern Antiquity) was reactivated as counter-memory in all the great legal revolutions of the modern world (Assmann 2015; Berman 1985).

It appears, however, that while such selections are ubiquitous in the modern order, there is a growing difficulty in modern society with respect to restabilization – as regards both systemic restabilization and rational reconstruction on a cognitive level, an issue that is also central to Habermas (1976; Weber 1978; Horkheimer and Adorno 1972). Modern world society often experiences itself as constructed, oscillating between contradictory selections and experiments with constant variations, at the expense of restabilization (i.e. temporary stability). The semantic promise is one of preadaptive advances, that is, the promise of a future in which, in accordance with individual taste, a global community integrated by, say, human rights or the Caliphate, or a world of neatly separated civilizations – such as the Russian world – is about to become reality. That is why, as Luhmann (2012: 296) put it, modern society encounters so many problems in distinguishing between restabilization and mere variation. This is arguably a key reason why such semantic promises are often prone to the use of violence and force in order to take a short-cut to the new order (for example a democratic or Islamic Middle East, a Russian-dominated post-Soviet space, etc.), as illustrated by the 2003 Iraq war or the rise and fall of Da'esh ('Islamic State') or Russia's war on Ukraine (2014/22). Seen from that perspective, and without making judgments about the ubiquity of variations in older societies, contemporary world society is experimenting with 'more and more daring disadaptations' (Luhmann 2012: 269), so that its evolution is characterized by nervous selections rather than restabilizations of expectations. Because experimentalism (Dewey 1925) goes hand in hand with rationalization, experiments with disadaptations are used methodologically in reflexive reiterations (see Foucault 2003). This links the innovative character of variation with the risk of daring social experiments, from eugenics to educational reforms, system crashes and legitimization crises that caution against equating systemic operations with order, functionalism and stability, let alone moral superiority.

3.2 Cognitive and normative evolution: Learning and unlearning

We need to reiterate at this point that the underlying distinction between social, cognitive and natural evolution does not pertain to the form of evolution (the sequence of variation, selection and restabilization) itself, but rather to the possible specifications of that form in three different contexts: the social world (social evolution), consciousness/mind systems (cognitive evolution), and biological or non-biological systems, such as the cosmos or tectonic plates (natural evolution). Each of these are characterized by fundamentally different constitutive elements and patterns which prohibit a simple copy and paste of the specifics of the form of evolution in one realm to another realm, although notable similarities exist (such as, for example, in relation to learning which is possible in both social and cognitive evolution, but different in each).[6] Moreover, despite the constitutive differences, they do not break with the continuum of evolution. There is some kind of internal connection between differently constituted evolutions in matter, organisms, societies and subjects.

'Being-in-the-world' (Heidegger 1993: §§ 12–18) connects the social with individually attributable, cognitive evolution (consciousness). When we think about drinking a beer, about who we are

---

6   In this respect, it makes little sense to argue about whether it is useful to 'apply' one kind of evolution to a specific realm, such as, most notably, 'world politics'. Usefulness in this case depends entirely on the understanding of how such a realm is constituted. If someone were to argue that world politics is not about communication or minds but about genes, then applying theories of natural evolution would make perfect sense – but it would also amount to saying that international politics resembles a violet or a sparrow.

and want to be or about evolutionary theory, in each case there is nothing meaningful, no knowledge in our head, in neverland or anywhere else. What is and occurs in our head can be observed from outside our consciousness and thinking (and with no participation from our consciousness at all). What the neuro-scientist observes is completely meaningless for the object of his or her observation: binary-coded neuronal storms. These storms can be observed only by high-tech scientists in a lab, and they have nothing to do with what we think about ourselves, about these storms and how we do that. Neuronal processes are self-referential but cannot think and reflect what they are doing, because thinking is acting (Kant 1968: §§ 15, 17), and acting is 'always already' acting in the world, which is a social 'lifeworld' following the path of the social evolution (Heidegger 1993: § 18; Husserl 1976: 111–113). Therefore, all acts of solitary thinking are speech acts. All we know, doubt or just think about is out there in the social world, and we are part of it, and so is thinking. Because: No thinking without thinking by using language, silently or aloud. There is no thought beyond present and moving human bodies (Strawson 1972). Abstract thought and theories exist frozen in artifacts, in libraries, on hard disks in space and time, but only in the state of latency (therefore Parsons rightly speaks of a latency system), whose conditions of manifestation are physically present readers.

Second, there is also a kind of internal relation between sociocognitive evolution (or the coevolution of subject and society) on the one hand, and the natural evolution of organisms, observed by natural scientists and philosophers at least since the mid-eighteenth century. Around 1800 it seemed to become ever more evident, as in the speculative evolutionary philosophy of Friedrich W. J. Schelling, and especially in his *Weltalter* fragments of 1811 and 1813 (Schelling 1946), that everything spiritual is modified physical impulse. Urge (in German: *Drang*) is, according to Schelling's insight the pre-form of spirit ('*Vorform von Geist*')' – and spirit here should already be read in its Hegelian meaning of subjective, objective and absolute spirit that means individual consciousness, society and culture (scientific, aesthetic, religious spheres of value) (Adorno 1975). Eighty years later Charles S. Peirce (1991) was already able to rely on a cruel biological experiment to verify Schelling's philosophical speculation. For Peirce 'absolute spirit' consists inter alia in logical reasoning, inferential operations, etc., underpinning a kind of behaviour and habit that ranges from animals like frogs to the propositionally differentiated use of language that has been observed only in the linguistic activities of human organisms. The hind legs of a frog 'severed from the rest of the body' do, 'when pricked, ... infer' from the pain, take flight and try to jump off (Peirce 1991: 201). The evolutionary idea that connects speculative idealism, young Hegelianism and American pragmatism of the nineteenth century is that material, physical, chemical, organic and cognitive processes occur in the same world as ideas, propositions, thoughts and inferences, relating the social, subjective and natural worlds to one another internally. Abductive, 'synthetic inferences' thus have 'a *fundamentum in re*' (Habermas 1991a: 28).

There are more differences: firstly, the fact that in social evolution and the cognitive evolution of consciousness there can be cognitive and normative evolution, whereas in natural evolution this is impossible. If there is a kind of learning in natural evolution before the evolution of primates, say for trees, mushrooms, dinosaurs, birds or mammals, then 'learning' can only be ascribed retrospectively to the display of genetically fixed capacities. However, there is recent research on epigenetic and behavioural learning processes which go beyond the mere display of genetically fixed capacities (Jablonka and Lamb 2014; Moore 2015).[7] For instance, English blue tits, which in the 1940s learned (and later unlearned after the way milk is bottled and

---

7   This is an important, indirect form of motivating others to learn to do what you can do yourself, that is, of teaching. In the case of imitation learning, which is 'relatively rare' in the animal world, but which occurs in songbirds, whales and zebra mongooses, protective enabling of educational behavior is even supplemented by teaching through active demonstration. The mongooses organize themselves in small hunting groups, in which the juvenile gang leaders teach the offspring to crack large hard-shelled eggs. Since the offspring can only do this through a mixture of construction and (constructively limited) chance (trial and error), there is a pluralization of different cracking cultures even within a community (Jablonka and Lamb 2014: 164,

delivered changed) by observation, trial and error, to open milk bottles capped with aluminum foil in order to eat the accumulated fat cream on top of the milk, passed on what they had learned to their offspring by restraining themselves and preventing the adolescents from taking the work and the food from the little ones. In this way, they ensured the latter a sheltered space in which they could teach themselves to peck through the bottletops by trial and error (Jablonka and Lamb 2014: 163). The black rats who found their way to the pine forests of Jerusalem in search of food learned in a similar way to extract the tasty pine nuts from the cones, using a similar pedagogic of indirect, student-centred instruction to pass what they had learned to their offspring (Jablonka and Lamb 2014: 169). There are only a few animals that can imitate others, such as songbirds, whales and zebra mongooses. In the latter case observers have noted that mongooses supplement student-centred (saving sheltered space for self-instruction) with teacher-centred instruction (by demonstration and imitation; Jablonka and Lamb 2014: 164, 171, 422f).

However, cases in which genetically fixed capacities meet a complex social environment are rare. Cases are not complex enough because of a lack of linguistic communication and complex forms of society formation, and they are never made explicit for the actors themselves. In general, learning by future generations through teaching, or transmission by tradition and socialization is absent. Punctuational bursts or tipping-points play a very different role in social as opposed to natural evolution. Though punctuational bursts are not impossible in natural evolution (as a result of, for example, meteorite strikes), revolutions – including technological breakthroughs – form an anticipated and systematic element of social evolution only, as we have highlighted above with regard to negation-driven changes to existing orders from early civilization through the four Axial Ages.[8] This is a pattern that has had a major

---

170f, 422f) The latter can often be observed in big ape societies too (Boesch 2012).

8   This anticipation mostly pertains to the expectations that revolutions will continue to take place and technological breakthroughs will continue to happen rather than an anticipation of their content or effects.

impact on world politics since the onset of complex forms of human civilization, from the pre-Axial Age era until today.

How can we explain the differentiation between normative and cognitive evolution in human subjects and societies? This differentiation seems to be constitutive for humans and their societies. However, there is still a continuum of change and learning that can explain punctuational bursts and tipping points not only by natural catastrophes (such as food crises, protein shortage or climate change) but also by crises, conflicts and contradictions that are internal to human societies and due to the language-based communicative forms of the social integration of growing disintegration (internal complexity).[9]

In this context, chimpanzee language is a key that opens the evolutionary continuum and explains the gap that divides human from big ape societies. All big apes (like many big animals) have a rich emotional 'language'. Big apes regularly perform grooming reciprocally. Moreover, chimps are more inclined to share their prey after reciprocal fondling and grooming. In particular, if chimps have recently been cuddled by others and freed from fleas and other mischief, their empathy grows (Muller and Mitani 2005: 275–331; Olsen 1997: 114). No doubt, chimps are feeling, emotional, empathic animals, who even show a kind of compassion as Darwin and Kropotkin famously observed. To a certain extent, chimps are sentimental animals, as are humans. However, they seem to have no moral consciousness, no sense of justice and they cannot accept or – even more importantly – deny reciprocally binding norms. They have no normative expectations and no normative obligations. They feel no normative pressure at all (and therefore cannot suffer from egoism), since they can perform reciprocal empathy, but cannot state and establish what they perform. They cannot deliberate and talk about their reciprocal relations – either factually or (even more important) counterfactually. But they can talk and produce cultural diversity to a certain extent.

---

9   See the interesting interpretation of Hegel's philosophy of law by Gurisch 2023. Luhmann describes the integration of disintegration as 'die noch zusammenhaltbare Ungleichheit' – the diversity that can still be held together (Luhmann 2019: 25).

They learn socially from others but cannot reverse or generalize what they have learned. Therefore, they can preserve it only as performative know-how, not as informative know-that in cultural memory. They can draw the attention of others to what they want to have, do or eat, but not show it to others or share knowledge of facts with others. It follows that they cannot divide their attention and teach their kids what they themselves have learned (or at best they can do so only in a rudimentary fashion). 'Divided attention is a trait specific to the human race' (Greenwood 2015: 119). Unlike spectators at a football game, chimpanzees never 'focus their attention on the same event because they cannot play and exchange social roles. They coordinate their actions with their group mates, but they cannot understand their interactions as self-made roles independent of behavior [i.e., abstract or abstracted] and therefore interchangeable. This is exactly what only humans can do so far, and this is what all cooperative activities are based on' (Greenwood 2015: 119).

There is an astonishing cognitive use of different but meaning-identical symbols in chimpanzee societies, and an even more astonishing increase in apes learning ever more symbolic communication, since for a couple of generations a lot of them have lived in hybrid societies where 'modern-day apes interacting with cooperative humans' is part of their everyday life (Tomasello 2008: 193). In homogenous as well as in hybrid societies, apes regularly use different symbolizations for the same imperative speech-act – for example, if a male chimp wants sex, he can direct his pointer (pointing gesture) to his erect member (A), and if that does not work, he can hit a bush with his front paws (B), and if that fails too he can use a third gesture (C), or reverse the order (C-B-A) or use any combination of symbolic gestures B-C-A etc. He may also learn and use even more gestures which are equivalent to one another (A=B=C). The same applies if a chimp wants something to eat from others, in particular humans.

At this level, the ability of the big apes to abstract (from the specific form of their gesture) is nearly the same as for humans, whereas the ability to perform speech acts is not. The apes can understand and perform only imperative speech acts reciprocally, and negate (or neglect) them or follow them but only through their behavioural reaction, not symbolically. Some other speech acts, especially informative ones they can understand and accept only from the point of view of the recipient. But they cannot negate them. They can understand the informative message, but not pass it on as a speaker because as a speaker they cannot dissolve the propositional content from the form of the speech act. They only can express their imperative request to get what the human pointing finger promises. Because they cannot inform each other reciprocally, they cannot chat and gossip (the most unique and important human characteristics). This is the crucial point that explains why they cannot reverse roles, cannot take an impartial third-party position, cannot construct counterfactual alternatives to either their individual or their social form of life hypothetically (Boehm 2001: 187–191). Therefore, they cannot make the rules they follow as rules explicit (and only through this explication do the rules become rules that – unlike genetic programmes – constitute a new formation of society) (Brandom 1994). They can demand food from others but see no reason, no need, no obligation to give food to another if the other wants or needs it. They can demand sex from others but see no reason to have sex if the other demands it. Demanding is the only role they can play reciprocally but without any kind of reciprocally binding obligation. If a researcher points to food which the apes could not have perceived before, they come and grab it. If she points to a vessel which hides the food with the same intention of helping them, they get the information that there is a vessel, hence they get the pointing intention but never get the helping intention. They even get hidden intentions, but only instrumental and imperative ones (Tomasello 2008: 14, 18, 26–30, 37–40, 202–206). Therefore, they cannot cooperate beyond the display of their genetic programme. But, and this is the closest point they reach to transgressing the border to becoming human, they can learn in hybrid societies to cooperate with humans; however, they cannot when they are only among themselves (Tomasello 2008: 193).

It is precisely at this point that the normative evolution of individual human subjects (1) and their society (2) departs from the cognitive evolution. What finally makes the difference on both levels is the turn from deviant, negating and resisting behaviour to explicit negation and contradiction. In individual and social evolution variation is exclusively brought about 'through a communication rejecting communication content' (Luhmann 1997: 461). This rejection contradicts 'the expectation of acceptance or simply an assumed continuity of "as always"' (ibid.). Without the 'daily mass production of deviant, unexpected, surprising communication,' that is, of 'contradiction' (and only if the communication is understood *as* contradicting) 'not in the logical, but in the more original dialogical sense' (ibid.). Only if the evolutionary pool of variation is stuffed with negation can human social evolution take off. This is the 'tremendous power of the negative' (Hegel 1952: 29). The socially 'existing contradiction' (Hegel 1975: 59; Hegel 1970: 332).

Normative evolution of the subject

In a well-known experiment a biologist cheats an ape to whom he often gives food with some inedible fake nuts. After a couple of tries the chimp gets the hidden cheating intention (that belongs to the inferential network of instrumental and imperative speech acts that the apes make use of reciprocally: they can cheat, and they understand when they are cheated). Then she (or he) will throw the fake nuts aggressively back at the biologist. This looks exactly like moral resentment, but it is not, at least not yet (Strawson 1962: 187–211). Apes and crows can cheat but not lie, because lying presupposes the informative use of symbols, cooperation, understanding how to help each other, having normative expectations and obligations etc. (Tomasello 2008: 202; Boehm 2001: 187–191). Therefore, the ape's (for us) highly understandable outburst of rage was still a Schellingian-Adornian impulse, a pre-form of *Geist* and normativity.

The crucial step from the pre-form of the *Geist* of normativity to the form itself is made at the moment when a small human child gets a small piece of cake and her big sister gets a big one, and the small kid asks: 'Why do I get a smaller piece?' This question opens a new discourse that splits off the normative evolution of the subject from its cognitive evolution.

However, this division is evidently only possible through the informative use of symbols and the entire network that hangs on it. It enables the step from impulse to protest, from resistance to contradiction, from deviant behaviour to negations and negative statements, from unwillingness to be dominated to a sense of injustice. 'Very often it is the injustice suffered that brings the laws of equality to consciousness' (Piaget 1973: 311). The little girl was right. By evoking the laws of equality, she jumped right into the centre of normative thinking. Equality can be conceptually defined as the negation of natural or primordial differences, accompanied by moral resentment: outrage at the injustice of unequal treatment, based on 'distinction of any kind, such as race, colour, sex, language, religion, political or other opinion, national or social origin, property, birth or other status.' (Art. 2 Universal Declaration of Human Rights 1948; Tugendhat 2007: 137–139). It is here that the normative evolution of the subject meets the normative evolution of society.

Normative evolution of society

There is some evidence that brother or sister chimpanzees (in rare but significant cases) are able to stage successful insurgencies against alpha despots and overcome the hierarchical structure of their society for some considerable time (between one and 20 years). During this time, they establish a kind of egalitarian brotherly rule over the female animals (as observed in a few highly significant cases in the wilderness of Gombe National Park, Tanzania), or an egalitarian sisterly rule over the male herd (as observed in two cases, one in Arnhem Zoo in the Netherlands, the other one in Yerkes National Primate Research Center, Georgia, USA). In every case the primary goal was to prevent a return to the hierarchical rule of a former alpha-despot, or the rise of a new one (i.e. a 'counterrevolution') (Boehm 2001: 187–189, 237f, 252f; Muller and Mitani 2005; Goodall 1986; Wilson 2012: 366).

What seems unique in the case of chimps is the change in societal structure from despotic hierarchy to egalitarian cooperation with flat hierarchies between sexes. An explanation might be that chimps not only have the cognitive capacity to abstract from the different symbols for the same things (demands), they can also, it seems, use their cognitive capacity to detach or abstract themselves to some extent from the close ties that bind their cooperation with genetic programmes of hunting and collective struggle (status, war etc.), and use the same schema of cooperation for various other (i.e. new) applications in insurgencies and, even more astonishingly, for cooperative suppression of a rising alpha despotism over a longer period of time, and to stabilize a kind of isonomia between the ruling half of the herd (that seen from afar resembles the relationship between the huge male, armed, and to a great extent slave-owning and 'democratically' ruling elite in ancient Athens and the rest of the population).

In all cases of successful insurgencies, the apes coordinate their own actions through socially learned gestures and a variety of challenging and angry Waa-vocalizations, and stabilize their egalitarian brotherly or sisterly life by a significant increase in reciprocal grooming, fawning, and other expressions of mutual sympathy that reinforce their sense of belonging and represent some pre-evolution of communicative coordination of action. This type of communication does not, however:

> permit the sharing of detailed behavior profiles, or the exchange of specific information in tracking individuals and watching for incipient signs of deviance, or discussions of what constitutes a desirable political milieu. A definitive reversal of the flow of power in bands requires some kind of vision of the kind of political society that is desired (Boehm 2001: 187).

This is the limit which the apes cannot transgress. Even if the Arnhem female chimps were:

> operating on an intentional basis, so they may be said to have goals – perhaps even 'values' insofar as the goals seem to be shared. They regularly cut down the power of males and circumscribe their roles, a pattern reminiscent of sanctioning and social control. However, their behavior preferences remain implicit in their behavior; in the absence of spoken symbolic language, they can neither formalize their behavioral preferences into a 'moral code' nor exchange detailed information about the deviant behavior of which they disapprove' (Boehm 2001: 188f).

Hence, the apes can carry out a successful insurgency, but not a revolution that produces new political institutions and ensures that the new semi-egalitarian societal formation is passed on to the next generation. They fail to make the step from Camus to Sartre, from revolt to revolution, indeed, they do not even show any interest in this step, because it is not in their world. Chimps can live without domination, but neither of them can signal to the other as graffiti in Berlin once did: *Anarchie ist machbar, Herr Nachbar!* (Anarchy is doable, dear neighbour!). Since they lack an informative, gossipy and argumentative, contentious and polemical use of language, they lack access to the tremendous power of the negative, and thus access to counterfactual, hypothetical, projective and evaluative thinking. Consequently, they cannot compare the new societal formation with the old or construct a mythical counter-memory of a successful uprising.

But this is exactly how a number of important ethnologists explain the emergence and the extremely long duration (between 200,000 and 25,000 years[10]) of egalitarian, acephalous small societies, which Christopher Boehm and others have described strikingly as reverse-dominance hierarchies: as societies which are organized in an egalitarian way in order to prevent the return of alpha-despotism, whether historical or mythically constructed – in other words, to prevent the counterrevolution (Boehm 2001, 1993: 227–240; Woodburn 1982: 431–451: 163).[11] In the reverse-dominance hierarchy of these societies, there must still have been alive a warningly remembered reference to an original dominance hierarchy that was overcome, overthrown, turned into its progressive opposite some time ago in the grey past (Knauft 1991: 391–428; Boehm 2001: 87; Sigrist 1994: 41). Moreover, if we take Pierre Clastres' (1974) work on war between egalitarian societies into account, then we can see that these wars are primarily anti-statist and anti-imperial wars. They are not aimed at conquest or building a hierarchical state or an empire, but at preventing state and empire-building in

---

10 The numbers are highly controversial, cf. Hauser, Chomsky and Fitch 2002: 1569–1579.

11 See also: Morris 2014: 22–37; Cashdan 1980: 116–120; cf. the debate with critics and Boehm's reply (Boehm 1993: 240–254).

order to ensure a permanent suspension of hostilities. In terms of Christopher Boehm's (1993) pathbreaking research, these societies were, thus, organized both internally ('nationally') and externally ('internationally') as such 'reverse dominance hierarchies'.

With the construction of this memory the coevolution of the cognitive and normative evolution of society began. Scriptless egalitarian and acephalous societies of hunters and gatherers stigmatized domineering relations by 'burning the law of equality, the prohibition of arrogance, into the body of the initiate' (Clastres 1974: 159). The disciplinary society was co-original with the normative evolution of egalitarian freedom, but the counter-memory reminded the disciplinary subject that the revolution against real or mythical alpha-despots can be repeated should they appear again, that it can be repeated in the event of the evolutionary emergence of a completely new formation of imperial class-rule by literate and educated slaveholders, and that it can be repeated against a disciplinary society that stabilizes their egalitarian freedom at a price that might be too high.

3.3 Core evolutionary concepts: Autonomization, hierarchical complexity and coevolution

Focusing on social evolution, its formal logic is defined by a sequencing of variation, selection and restabilization, deeply grounded in social structure and history, that rests on the inseparability between communications as society's basic units and its social structures understood as communication-based systems. Thus, over time – through reiterated communications – systems with specific properties and internal power dynamics emerge as an effect (and, as noted, a boundary condition) of this sequencing. This also relates to world politics, as a social realm with distinct socially constructed (and therefore non-static) systemic properties (Albert 2016). We therefore distinguish analytically between the formal logic of sequencing and systemic properties, while highlighting that, from the paradigmatic perspective of constructivist theory, they are inherently interwoven. These systemic properties boil down to a complex yet clearly defined social ontology that allows world politics to be conceived of as part of what Luhmann (2000) refers to as the system of politics understood as a non-linear social realm (Albert 2016). Three key structural effects are often highlighted in social evolution theories indebted to the paradigmatic tradition to which we have recourse, namely the 'autonomization of levels' (Stichweh 2002), the coevolution of these levels and, finally, their internal 'hierarchical complexity' (Commons and Ross 2008; Vrba and Gould 1986). We will further illustrate how these three structural dimensions of social evolution affect world politics in what follows. We begin by outlining their theoretical rationale, and in this context, it is important to re-emphasize that we see world politics as a realm in which, as in every other social realm, there is always both structural evolution and an evolution of ideas/semantics. This follows from our general take on the connection between social evolution and social evolutionary theory. It is impossible to have one without the other.[12]

In the context of world politics as a distinct social realm, autonomization relates to the emergence and restabilization of politics as a self-referential social system that evolves in relation to other social systems, such as law, economy, religion, science, etc. Autonomization highlights the decoupling, however precariously, of politics from society-wide logics of segmentation or stratification – although these forms of differentiation may very well endure as system-internal forms (first and foremost in the strong forms of stratification and hierarchy in world politics over much of its history during the last two or three centuries, for instance between great powers and other units, or between the West and the Global South; Zarakol 2017; Stetter 2008). It is about what we mean when we say that international politics or world politics is 'systemic', a widespread claim in IR but not always backed up by an understanding of systemic properties sufficiently embedded in social theory. From a general theoretical perspective that looks at society as a whole, autonomization thus addresses the increasing complexity (not be mistaken for a simplistic distinction between 'primitive' and 'civilized') at the level of social order from hunter-gatherer

---

12   See Preyer 1998 for an attempt to describe the evolution of a world system in terms of structural evolution only.

societies after the invention of language (and before the Neolithic revolution around 9000 BCE), via hierarchical empires and centre-periphery societies following the diffusion of writing since the end of the fourth millennium, to the modern, functionally differentiated world society, that was arguably stabilized by the invention of book printing in the course of the second millennium CE and the telegraph during the nineteenth century. As Luhmann and others (including Habermas) have shown, this integration of society within an overarching, yet internally differentiated order is accompanied by a growing tendency of social systems to function according to self-referential logics, entailing growing internal differentiation. Luhmann (1995: 34–36) uses the term 'autopoiesis', but 'autonomization' is more widely used. This autonomization of social systems in human history undergirds the evolution from hunter-gatherer communities (which knew only one system, namely tribes), via Neolithic segmentary communities to stratified classes (that relied on two mutually exclusive strata based on personal properties – ruling class versus subjects and slaves). Emergent world society then produced a theoretically unlimited number of autonomous social systems, such as politics, law, religion, economics, sports, art, science, etc. – and distinct subsystems such as a world political system in the context of the autonomous system of politics. These systems are, as far as their logic of reproduction is concerned, decoupled from personal properties and differentiated internally (Albert and Buzan 2010).

Hierarchical complexity refers to the way in which systems at a new stage of evolution accommodate previous forms, for example the various ways in which earlier forms such as segmentation, stratification and centre-periphery differentiation permeate functional differentiation. We have noted above that world politics as a system that is functionally differentiated from other social realms through internal differentiation accommodates a wide variety of other forms of differentiation, such as segmentation into like units and stratification based on hierarchical power differences, as well as functional differentiation (e.g. international regimes). Hierarchical complexity also shares many characteristics with Foucault's archaeology of knowledge, which also stresses how discursive formations integrate the 'antecedents' (Foucault 1972: 143) into a given regime

3 Contemporary social evolution and social evolutionary theories 77

of truth. The antecedent is 'subordinated to the discourse' (ibid.) and is integrated on the basis of a hierarchical logic that 'may also involve a temporal vector' (ibid.: 168). However, at the same time its traces cannot be eradicated. Antecedents shape the manifold bifurcations and contradictions that undergird the *épistème* as well as the 'discontinuities, ruptures, gaps, [and] entirely new forms of positivity' (ibid.: 169), that any social form encounters and that have to be integrated into a critical theory of power in social evolution, as Tang (2013: 137) observes. Finally, and taking into account the aforementioned coevolution of society and consciousness, theories of social evolution emphasize increasing complexity at the normative level, a characteristic unique to social evolution. We refer here to changes in normative constraints as, for example, postulated in Kant's cosmopolitan reflections, in Elias's theory of civilization (Linklater 2016) and particularly in Habermas's approach to the evolution of society (Habermas 2020: 139, 862; McKitrick 1993).

Coevolution refers to the way in which an autonomous system (or subsystem) of this kind relates to another system as an environment that is relevant to the reproduction of them both, for example how a social system relates to the human psyche or to the natural world (Diamond 2005), or how a social system like politics relates to another social system such as law (thereby again pointing to significant overlaps between Luhmann and Habermas, e.g. inasmuch both address the coevolution of politics and law; Brunkhorst 2014). The power and knowledge nexuses identified by Foucault can also be understood as features of coevolution, as in Foucault's (2008) treatment of the early Christian Church. Reproduction in the neo-Darwinian theory of evolution is thus not a muscular ability to outlive others in a struggle for the survival of the fittest. Belief in what Stichweh (2002: 10) characterizes as an 'eliminative confrontation of a system with its environmental constraints' is outdated. Contemporary theories of evolution prefer to highlight the random forms of often precarious adaptation, the contingency and non-linearity of change, as well as a great deal of non-functionality on the part of structures in relation to their environment. One example would be the growing emphasis on 'risks' and 'disorder' in modern society and the ubiquity of 'contingent local adaptations' (Stichweh 2002: 22), such as the decoupling between world culture and concrete local practices (Meyer 2000). Another example would be shifts in the prevalent forms of power as studied by Foucault, from sovereign and disciplinary forms of power, for example, to those that are particularly central to modern social orders, such as governmental power, which hinges on much more indirect strategies of maintaining and challenging political authority. As highlighted above, coevolution also encompasses the relationship between social forms and consciousness. This is why social evolution understood in this way does not lead simply to some kind of unconstrained flow of cognitive learning, but also to normative learning processes that might result in prophetic moral universalism, human rights legislation or the 'modern cult of the individual', as in Foucault's notion of technologies of the self in the context of governmental power (compare Durkheim 1933; Jung and Stetter 2018). Normative learning leads to a specific form of conditioned adaptation in which adaptive improvement can be normatively constrained: 'not justice has to submit to adaptation but adaptation has to submit to justice' (Brunkhorst 2014: 36). Therefore, normative learning, as Adler (2019: 29) observes as well, puts constraints on selective processes and adaptive improvements. All these diverging forces, paradoxical imperatives, fragmented regimes and contradictory interests, together with normative constraints thereby influence, modify and limit the selective processes and changing directions of social evolution.

These core evolutionary concepts may be focused on individually or be used as a kind of prism in order to analyse a specific evolutionary process or a specific aspect of one. In order to sharpen understanding of what these concepts mean, this is the way that we will be using them in the empirical applications from world politics that follow. However, it is important to point out that focusing on, for example, autonomization, does not mean that there will be no hierarchical complexity present. This is a point that we will take up in each of the individual illustrations in the next chapter. As this also means zooming in on more 'traditional' subjects within the purview of International Relations, we need firstly to discuss and relate to the various ways in which (theories of) evolution have been used in approaches circumscribed by various disciplines.

3.4 Existing approaches to evolution in IR

Mere use of the word 'evolution' in IR contexts does not necessarily say anything about explicit engagements with (theories of) social evolution. Quite often 'evolution' is used loosely and interchangeably with concepts like 'development', 'emergence', or 'change'. We are not addressing these approaches here, only referring to instances where use of 'evolution' points to a specific quality of change in world politics, which allows for the evolutionary steps of variation, selection and restabilization.

Upon first inspection, this clearly pertains to works that consider evolution in world politics by analogy with, and with direct reference to, evolution in the natural world, whether at the level of species or that of individual genes or neuronal synapses (Johnson 2015). Though these contributions seem to be gaining some purchase in the discipline, we can dismiss them here essentially for the two reasons already mentioned: because theories of natural evolution cannot account for processes of social, cognitive and normative evolution, which necessarily require and are characteristic of complex *social* contexts; and because they have difficulties in accounting for the tipping points characteristic of social systems, namely instances of revolutionary change. Theories of natural evolution in IR tend to focus on the change of actors and units. By doing so, however, they overemphasize the role of actors as triggers of evolution, ignoring the fact that the basic unit of evolution in social systems is not actorhood, but rather, as we will show in more detail below, discourse, communication and practice – in other words those social forms that engender meaningful social actorhood in the first place (Meyer and Jepperson 2000). It is only through a focus on the social evolution of discourse, communication and practice that actors can be related to the broader social environment in which change takes place, for example with respect to changing notions of actorhood within a system triggered by cognitive and normative evolution (see Luhmann 2012; Wendt 2015). Put differently, not only do states, as a particularly important kind of actor, evolve – they also reflect on this. We do not conclude from this, however, that theories of natural evolution would be of no use for IR: quite the contrary, they can be put to good use if properly applied. They already come into play indirectly, as many theories of natural evolution nowadays challenge the very idea that natural laws are absolute and beyond history. A broad stream of scientific theories from microphysics via theories of the evolution of the universe (Pape 1994; Hampe 2010) to general systems theory, quantum theory and thermodynamics (Nicolis and Prigogine 1987) back the idea that not only the presumed natural laws governing the human realm (Morgenthau 1946), but even the natural laws of physics undergo change (Unger and Smolin 2014). Due to mechanisms of accidental variation and evolutionary change, theories of natural evolution also keep space open for freedom of action (Wartenberg 1971; Pape 1994). Theories and analyses of natural evolution also come into play directly when the goal is to analyse the relation between social and natural evolution, for example how bioclimatic conditions on the islands of Japan were one precondition for the rise of Japanese culture, including its foreign relations (Diamond 2005), or how climate change affected political constellations, for example during the Little Ice Age in the late middle ages and early modernity. However, the important point here is that in order to make use of theories of natural evolution, it is necessary to first come to terms with the specificity of social evolution. Only then can both concepts of evolution be related to each other. Directly applying theories of natural evolution that cannot account for cognitive and normative learning and revolutionary change, to realms primarily characterized by these very processes, or considering actors and not communications, discourse and practice as the basic unit of evolution, constitutes a theoretically unwarranted shortcut.[13]

There are, arguably, very few studies on the nature of, and change in, world politics in IR without at least an implicit account of social evolution. The lines here zigzag, as the role that individual approaches, explicitly or implicitly, bestow on social evolution depends entirely on the primary analytical frames of reference used.

---

13   And it should be noted that, in our view scandalously, this shortcut is regularly taken by completely ignoring even the existence of theories of social evolution.

It makes a big difference whether social evolution is seen to pertain to the basic structures of the international system, or just to cognitive learning in specific settings of foreign-policy decisionmaking. Taking a non-evolutionary stance regarding the main analytical frame of reference usually does not preclude conceding social evolution on other levels. Thus, for example, while a Waltzian international system is clearly conceived in structural-functional and non-evolutionary terms as regards system structure (Goddard and Nexon 2005), it knows bounded evolution in terms of polarity and could easily concede that social evolution happens below the systemic level. In fact, it could be argued that some view of 'bounded evolution' is characteristic of a range of approaches in the realist tradition. While invariably based on a strong conception of things that do not change – universal laws to be found throughout history such as anarchy or the nature of human beings – there has always been a strong trait in realism that emphasizes that this lack of change on a grand scale does not preclude variation going on all the time and that, for this reason, specific events and pathways cannot be 'calculated'.[14] Machiavelli states that things are 'different' in Siena from the way they are in Florence, and in a famous exchange on whether repetition facilitates theorizing or not, Morgenthau states that 'both [Martin] Wight´s and my orientation are historical, and it is this historical orientation that sets us apart from the present fashionable theorising about international relations' (Morgenthau 1970: 251). Social evolution cannot change the laws of nature or of the human realm, but it takes place within the boundaries set by them. Old-school realists, even when in search of 'general causes', remain 'conscious of the role accidents play in history' (Morgenthau 1946: v). What Morgenthau seems to have in mind is something very close to evolutionary contingency and evolutionary tipping points.

While realists set general boundary conditions for the possibilities of social evolution, another prominent way of setting such conditions can be found, as we have already suggested, in the practice of assigning overarching importance to 'benchmark dates' that define international society. In benchmark date accounts, social

---

14 This was the main theme of the Second Great Debate in IR in the 1960s.

evolution may or may not occur, but such accounts start, by definition, with the idea of crucial interruptions, such 1648, 1789, 1919 or 1945. These dates were tipping points: things were different before as compared with the period after. While Buzan and Lawson (2014) in effect ask for a more evolutionary orientation and call for benchmark years to be de-emphasized, to focus instead on dates when nothing 'important' happened (according to a classical benchmarking rationale), they leave it open for others to explore whether and to what degree benchmark-date-oriented accounts contain inherent claims that benchmark dates are equivalent to 'revolutions' in theories of social evolution. They refer, for example, to 1860 as a benchmark date for international relations at which several nested processes intersected, such as rationalization, industrialization, technological change, modes of warfare, and ideological change (Bright and Geyer 2011). The degree to which benchmark dates thus defined are convincing can only be ascertained by looking more closely at individual studies. It seems quite likely, though, that those who rely on benchmark dates while putting them into historical context are more likely to be sensitive to more subtle evolutionary developments than are broad (and often dubious, see de Carvalho et al. 2011) statements about epochal differences such as 'Westphalian' vs. 'post-Westphalian'.[15]

It should be emphasized that the possibility of an implicit social evolution is also present in cases where IR studies operate with strong meta-historical narratives, that is, versions of a philosophy of history. Usually such narratives are normatively laden. They can invariably be found in cosmopolitanism and liberalism, and more generally where 'grand narratives' or narratives of progress are at work. One example would be Andrew Linklater's (2016) work that draws on Norbert Elias's theory of a process of civilization. The least normative, yet probably most explicitly teleological contribution in

---

15 From an evolutionary perspective, rather than speaking about benchmark dates it is more appropriate to speak about a 'threshold period' (*Sattelzeit*), as Reinhart Koselleck 2018) does when he postulates that most of our concepts were irrevocably transformed over the period 1750–1850.

that context is probably Alexander Wendt´s (2003) article on the inevitability of a world state.[16]

The most prominent role that evolution plays in IR analysis can probably be found in the field of research that deals with the emergence, development and spread of international regimes and norms (e.g. 'norm cycles'). These approaches share what Emmanuel Adler (1991), following Ernst Haas, has called an 'evolutionary epistemology', in which learning plays a central role underpinning change. Actors study the past, develop new cognitive models on that basis (variation) and put them into practice (selection), as John Ikenberry (2000) has argued in relation to great powers. Here, the design of post-conflict orders (restabilization) is based on cognitive reflection by new great powers about the failure of previous great powers to render past post-war orders durable. Still, even this explicit reference to evolution remains silent on the specificity of evolutionary mechanisms in the social world, a feature that it shares with other approaches in IR.

The fact that evolution is formally characterized by the three-step interplay of variation, selection and restabilization, even though, particularly in social and political matters, selection is, as we will outline in the next section, not the *only* mechanism of change (Gould 2002; Brunkhorst 2014) is, thus, often neglected, particularly in debates on the concept of learning. Most of the approaches mentioned above remain silent about these three central elements of evolution. They also remain silent about the basic unit of variation – a single, complete communicative speech act (or a single, complete symbolic gesture). Communicative operations (speech acts, gestures) are complete only through the affirmative or negative reply of an Alter Ego, and only negation (deviance) can trigger variation. This has been explained in linguistic theory from Humboldt to Chomsky over

---

16 Although it is not directly concerned with IR, Wendt's newest book (2015) clearly indicates that in the future he will be reinforcing this teleological view. It is remarkable that while in history, particularly as a result of 'global history', narratives of 'meta-history' and the philosophy of history are nowadays decidedly out of fashion (Rüsen 2014), they should still play such a prominent role in contemporary IR.

and over again, but only Luhmann and Habermas (both following the linguist Karl Bühler) have applied this linguistic discovery to the theory of social evolution, a necessary move, we maintain, given the centrality of language-based communication for human society. The key observation here then is that, in social evolution, communicative variation replaces genetic variation, and that is why communication, discourse and practice – not actors – are the basic units of social evolution, triggering a co-constitution of societal evolution and consciousness-related 'learning'.

It is on this basis that we argue that the 'value-added' of theories of social evolution is that they can help us understand changes within a complex social realm without relying on assumptions of fixed structures, ahistorical conditions, or causal laws within a system. And while there are vastly different opinions in the case of IR as to whether that complex social realm should be called an international system, a world society, an international political system or something else, all of these terms seem to allow for a much broader and systemic application of theories of social evolution that have been around in the social sciences for literally centuries, yet up to now have barely been registered explicitly by IR.

Our approach is certainly not the first to introduce a formal and explicit understanding of evolution. Within the discipline of IR alone, there is a huge body of literature that could be read as having at least implicit traces of accounts of social evolution, such as when Morgenthau discusses the need for a historical perspective on continuity and change in international politics and argues that, when in search of 'general causes', IR needs to remain 'conscious of the role accidents play in history' (Morgenthau 1946: v). However, these contributions almost always neglect the basic difference between the evolution of society as a highly complex social realm on the one hand, and the evolution of individual human psychological and biological features on the other. Neglecting this difference not only risks leading to biological reductionism but is usually also accompanied by a neglect of, if not outright ignorance about, the existence of a rich tradition of social evolutionary theorizing in the social sciences (see Lebow 2013), parts of which we discussed in the previous section. There are, as mentioned above, some scholarly works that think of evolution in world politics as analogous to evolution in the natural world, whether at the level of species or that of individual genes or neuronal synapses (Johnson 2015). We caution against taking this shortcut for the basic reason already highlighted that, while natural evolution matters for world politics as a boundary condition, it does not inform us about the way change occurs at the level of social systems, that is to say in realms that are not made up of biological elements such as cells or other organisms, but rather by social entities that possess the ability to reflect about their sociality.[17] In IR literature two other approaches in addition to ours can be discerned that have recently explicitly attempted to study world politics in terms of evolution.

Shiping Tang (2013; see also 2010 and 2020), in *The Social Evolution of International Politics*, offers an overview of a range of evolutionary approaches in IR, and shares with us the view that natural and social evolution need to be distinguished from one another. What sets Tang's approach apart from our own is his strong focus on an international system of states as the evolving system, whereas, for

---

17   Put differently: the direct application of theories of natural evolution to the study of social evolution commits a category error. It assumes a comparability of fundamentally different social and natural realms from the perspective of a theory of natural evolution, and overlooks the fact that the only thing that is shared by theories of social and natural evolution is something different, namely an 'elementary grammar of *every* theory of evolution' (Giesen and Schmid 1975: 394). There is a distinct, but small category of work in IR that explicitly deals with social evolution in world politics without falling into the trap of simply transplanting theories of natural evolution to the social world. A core contribution is by Jason Sharman (2014), who, on the basis of sociological institutional reasoning, highlights the centrality of selection dynamics in relation to the emergence of states as leading actors in the international system. However, he does not discuss the issues of communication and social ontology in any detail. Others, such as Thompson (2001) and Modelski and Devezas (2007), have provided intriguing evolution theory perspectives on world politics, but they differ from our approach in their consistent choice of states instead of communications and discourses as the main unit of analysis.

basic methodological reasons, we look at world politics not through the lens of a specific type of actorhood, but through specific forms of communication that engender notions of actorhood in the first place, a point completely missed by Tang (for an IR perspective on the social underpinnings of state-actorhood see Sharman 2014). Moreover, being focused on state-interactions, Tang does not engage in a wider discussion of the different mechanisms of power that operate in world politics beyond the quite simplistic realist notions of power from which he draws. So, for example, he refrains from juxtaposing different forms of power that are widely discussed in critical IR literature, including those, like governmental power and resistance, that highlight the wide range of spheres of world politics in which forms of power other than those related to offensive and defensive realism are in play. Moreover, in our view, privileging the state unnecessarily limits the analysis of the evolution of world politics, although it can possibly lead to similar empirical observations regarding certain specific issues. A second thing that concerns us about Tang's study is that it ultimately advances a teleological and quite Eurocentric perspective of world politics by distinguishing between a zero-sum world of (offensive) states from their first emergence, and an allegedly somewhat more cooperative (defensive) world that came into existence largely from the end of World War II. This is problematic not only because it replicates a Euro-centric (or Americo-centric) narrative, widely and rightly criticized in IR by historical-sociological (cf. Schlichte and Stetter 2023) and post-colonial scholarship, which Tang does not take into consideration (Seth 2011). It also contradicts a key insight in (biological) social evolutionary theory, namely that, while providing a handy illustration for textbooks, the view that evolution proceeds in neatly separated epochs has become outdated (Bourke 2011) and needs to be replaced by a perspective on the emergent properties of novel forms of (social) organization that is, for example, well captured by notions of hierarchical complexity (see below). Seen from that perspective, the core evolutionary mechanism is not the supposed change from one form of organizing anarchy to another, as Tang claims in the tradition of Bull (1977) and Wendt (1999), but the effects that an increasing autonomization of world politics has on the way in which this system operates.

In line with Tang's interest in different forms of social organization (e.g. offensive and defensive realist eras) it is important to note that, as regards structure, the theories of social evolution in the paradigmatic tradition that we draw upon are interested in both single events in the form of erupting contestations and in the *longue durée* of the emergence, change and 'death' of broader social structures in human history. Social evolution theories thus understood may be able to identify stages of structural evolution in society as well. However, in contrast to historicist epistemologies, which underpin Tang's argument about an alleged shift from offensive to defensive realism, social evolution theories should stress the non-linear character of evolution. Being more concerned with macro-structures – such as power-cycles – than with the formal sequencing of social evolution and how they are essentially intertwined with social effects (i.e. a flat social ontology), Tang's work is too detached from social theory and therefore basically reproduces theoretically questionable state-centric and teleological assumptions as far as social structure is concerned.

Communication, in a nutshell, is also what distinguishes social from cognitive evolution – the bedrock of Emanuel Adler's wide-ranging contribution to social evolutionary theory. Social evolution as defined in the previous section is about the evolution of social systems as, and through, communication. While both social and cognitive evolution operate on the basis of meaning, and although processes of learning are certainly possible in social systems, cognitive evolution is ultimately only possible in psychological systems (that is, to put it more conventionally, in individuals) that, according to Adler, group together in various communities of practice. For Adler, communities of practice rather than communications are the main carriers of evolution. While these communities of practice are embedded in, observe and address, and in turn are observed and addressed by, social systems, and while, therefore, cognitive evolution is widespread and significant, social systems themselves do not evolve cognitively. Cognitive evolution certainly has massive consequences for social evolution in terms of providing 'input' for variations, and in terms of conditioning the likelihood of selections, but, from the paradigmatic angle central to our argument, it is simply not social evolution (though, to be fair, based on the paradigmatic traditions he relates to, for Adler it is). However, given these linkages, it would be surprising if social and cognitive evolution were not closely related to each other and an analysis of changing forms of order did not often yield overlapping perspectives. It is in this sense that we think that, most notably, Adler's analysis and ours, although coming from different paradigmatic backgrounds and drawing on different sets of literature, can be related to each other. This also applies to the notion of a 'bounded idea of progress based on a common humanity' (Adler 2019: 5). We are, to be sure, sceptical of the idea that there is direct progress in evolution: both learning and unlearning are possible (Schmid 1998: 389). But we are in sympathy with Adler as far as an increasing complexity at the normative level is concerned, which figures, for example, in Elias's *longue durée* account of a process of civilization and is to be understood in our framework as the structural coupling between human consciousness and (communication-based) social systems. Despite highlighting (possible) similar outcomes here, we differ from Adler by separating these two dimensions. Adler, we would suggest, presents an analysis based neither on a theory of social evolution, nor one based directly on a theory of cognitive evolution, but rather offers a specific social theory that utilizes a theory of cognitive evolution.[18] That is also why our understanding of social evolution does not require us to highlight specific entities or agents as drivers or main subjects of evolution, as Adler (communities of practice) or Tang (states) do. We rather conceive of social evolution – and a possible advance in civilization – as a process that, through communications, engenders specific forms of actorhood to which agency is ascribed. In other words, we are putting forward a fundamentally constructivist understanding of actorhood all the way

---

18 Although this is a subject beyond the scope of this book, we assume that the theoretical bridge between Adler's social theory, which uses a theory of cognitive evolution and includes his previous work on practices, and a theory of social evolution, would be to account for practices as main subjects of social evolution (see Runciman 1998 and Müller 2010 on this in the context of other theories of social evolution).

down (Meyer and Jepperson 2000). The question then becomes how – under the condition of double contingency – forms of actorhood vary, get selected or deselected and restabilized and how, in specific social realms, communications are attributed to actors thus understood.

Another difference between Adler and ourselves pertains to the importance attributed to systemic factors. Adler identifies a cacophony of discourses triggered by a multitude of communities of practice in international politics. But he remains reluctant to define the encompassing structural characteristics of what we suggest is an autonomous system of world politics in which practices play out, suggesting instead that there is a mere 'plurality of international social orders' (Adler 2019: 137). While he concedes that social evolutionary theory has to be systemic, he refrains from embarking on systemic reasoning for most of his analysis, based on the somewhat paradoxical argument that, while he recognizes that the (cognitive) evolutionary theory he proposes is systemic, he wants to proceed 'without hardly invoking the concept of systems' (ibid: 9). Instead, he focuses on a multitude of communities of practice and on an evolutionary ontology that highlights 'becoming' and 'horizontal power' (ibid.: 45). While his study of cognitive evolution makes a great contribution to a better understanding of the emergence, consolidation and change of communities of practices – undoubtedly a central element in world politics – the driving ideas underpinning such communities and the competition between them, he remains conspicuously silent about their larger impact on world politics as a distinct social realm, including the arguably overwhelming centrality of vertical (i.e. hierarchical) power that has shaped this social realm, both historically and in the modern order (Mattern and Zarakol 2016). The reason for this is, arguably. that Adler attributes to notions of 'systems' or 'structures' a non-evolutionary and non-constructivist ontology of essence. While he appears to be particularly aware of Luhmannian systems theory, he fails to coherently engage with it and often misinterprets some of its key claims. This is evident in his cursory discussion of Luhmann. Besides not engaging systematically with Luhmann's social theory, Adler actually seems to be quite mistaken when claiming that Luhmann is not a 'theorist of becoming' and lacks a focus on 'continual transformation and flux' (Adler 2019: 62). We are confident that a closer reading of Luhmann invalidates such an argument. For, whatever else one makes of Luhmann's theory and the way it relates to world politics, it undoubtedly lays out a radically constructivist understanding of social systems as emergent and 'in flux', and of the ever-evolving societal effects of communication. Social systems, in other words, do not exist outside and independent from communication. In Adler's account, social order also appears as a realm defined by countless interrelated communities of practice, but he refrains from discussing overarching systemic properties. This is legitimate according to the paradigmatic approach from which he starts, but it raises the problem of the borders of this social order, a problem that both Luhmann and Habermas identified in quite similar ways (see above). Finally, a polycentric and pluralistic perspective on the multitude of communities of practice as highlighted by Adler is useful in and of itself, but it also means that he, like Tang, risks underestimating power, the system-wide hierarchies and the institutionalized power differences between concrete social groups (e.g. states vs non-states; the West vs the Global South; great powers vs others; security professionals vs lay people) that, we would argue, have come into being in the course of the evolution of world politics as a distinct social system (Zarakol 2017). Tang (2013: 37) correctly notes that the notion of cognitive evolution and the focus on multitudes of communities of practice leads to the problem that 'power and real conflict do not really feature' in Adler's theory – while ignoring that the same applies to his own account's under-complex theory of power. This then might be the reason why, not unlike Tang, Adler falls into a somewhat modernist narrative of progress, that might be understandable against the background of an ethical motivation, but is theoretically and historically questionable.

4 Evolutionary trajectories in world politics

The following illustrations of evolutionary trajectories in world politics are deliberately cast wide in the sense that they are decidedly *not* based on a fixed definition of what world politics 'is'. On the contrary. Social evolution is always about something being in the process of becoming and transforming – although there are certainly zones where things fizzle out in terms of being meaningful thus marking the, historically contingent, boundaries of a realm. This means that analysing something in terms of social evolution necessarily requires ontological openness. It is not about the evolution of something that somehow is, or was at some point, there in a fixed state, but something that is always evolving in terms of what it is, although that does include the distinct possibility of its being in historical zones marked by comparatively lower or higher levels of perturbation.

4.1 Forms of organizing political authority in the emergence and transformation of a modern system of world politics

It is possible to reconstruct the emergence and transformation of a modern system of world politics in terms of social evolution along the analytically distinct, yet factually inextricably linked dimensions of autonomization, hierarchical complexity and coevolution (the latter operating both internally, between different parts or subsystems of the system of world politics, and externally, particularly in its relation to the legal system). While such a reconstruction would not necessarily fix a completely exclusive and narrow understanding of what such a 'system' of world politics is, it would proceed on the basis of two central observations. Firstly, world politics (or, for that matter: 'international relations') is not something that evolved out of the interaction of 'units' that somehow existed previously and independently of it, at some point 'emancipating' itself from these units in the form of an emergent 'system' level with its own logic (structure, 'polarity', etc.). Secondly, for world politics to form a distinguishable social system it requires differentiation from other forms of politics (or/and from politics as an encompassing part of the social world distinct from the economy, religion, etc.). The latter means that, considering details of system definitions and the historical expression of processes of social differentiation, a system of world politics will not have emerged over night. Neither, quite certainly, will it have emerged completely 'out of time' and disentangled from accompanying processes of the functional differentiation of society, nor without an accompanying – if not necessarily simultaneously appearing – semantics for describing itself as 'world politics'. Nothing in this means that a system of world politics would have appeared out of nowhere. Quite the contrary. It built on the long evolutionary trajectories of the emergence (and also the disappearance) of structural as well as semantic elements and their associated symbolic codes (e.g. diplomacy, see 4.3 below), as well as on a contemporary practice of observation of self and others (in this case through the scientific practice of IR) that ensured the system's (relatively) 'smooth running' by relieving it from always having to consider its contingent past (either by its erasure or by constructing historical continuities).

This section will first take a look at this distinction between world politics as a system and its 'forerunners'. It will then briefly argue that some of the underlying evolutionary logic can also be found in some central contributions to IR, even in some rather unsuspected cases (here notably the 'structural realism' introduced by Kenneth Waltz). After that, it will discuss auto-nomization in terms of the evolution of particular system characteristics that centrally rely on the observational scheme of the balance of power; hierarchical complexity as the way in which this observational scheme manages to include a variety of forms of organizing political authority within itself; and coevolution particularly with the system of law, that, on the one hand, introduced complexity into the system by inserting normative restraints, while, on the other, hedging the hierarchical complexity mentioned by privileging one form of organizing political authority (the sovereign territorial state) over others (most notably 'formal' empires, but also, city-states, private authorities, emergent forms of world statehood, etc.).

It is certainly possible, and in many cases legitimate, to see world politics as only a somewhat loosely circumscribed realm whose existence can be traced back quite far in history, and then describe various trajectories of social evolution within such a realm (see Neumann and Glørstad 2022; and section 4.3 below on the proto-diplomatic practices that extend as far as prehistoric times). However, and in addition to individual evolutionary trajectories within such a realm, it is possible to trace the emergence of a distinct social system of world politics itself as an evolutionary outcome. These two things are closely related to each other, but they are not the same. They might be said to relate to each other in the way that, for example, the evolution of building practices relates to the evolution of cities. Building practices evolved well before, and continued to evolve further after, the invention of cities, and the latter had a decisive impact on what kind of buildings emerged thereafter and on ideas about, and the very practice of, architecture. However, a city as an identifiable sociospatial form can never be reduced to a mere assemblage of buildings (or other forms of dwellings), however complex. In order to become such a distinct form, it needs to differentiate itself from its environment on the basis not only of some kind of physical marker, but also of distinct codes and practices of organization.

Though operating on a very different timescale from the invention of cities, one could say that a system of world politics is to individual world political practices – however complex and historically deep these might be – what cities are to buildings. As will be discussed further below, there has been a long evolution of diplomatic practices in an overall generalized context of power competition. There have been diplomatic exchanges, conflicts, and other forms of interaction between what, for the sake of simplicity, can be summarized under the term 'polities' going on over millennia, that bear some formal if not substantive resemblance to what in contemporary times is usually summarized as 'international relations' between territorial (nation-)states (cf. Buzan and Little 2000, Buzan 2023). However, none of the historical 'precursors' to 'modern' international relations evolved into a system of world or international politics – at least, not if an at least moderately strict understanding of a system as requiring a clear distinction between the system and its environment is applied.[1] Many evolutionary paths can be identified, but they have not yet led to the emergence of a semantics of either 'international politics'/'international relations', or 'world' politics (the former emerging slowly from the beginning of the nineteenth century, the latter only as a latecomer in the context of other 'world' composite terms – world sport, world literature, world time, etc. – late in that century), *nor* to a distinct social system clearly differentiated from its environment. Interactions between polities, that were very often also organized as intra- or inter-familial/dynastic relations (cf. Haldén 2020; also Montefiore 2023) took place all the time, but they became 'world politics' (or, but only with the increasing merger of the ideas of territorial statehood and national belonging into the idea of nation-statehood in the late nineteenth and early twentieth centuries, *international* relations) only through the differentiation and autonomization of a system of world politics. Autonomization in this sense means that world political communication can be easily identified as such and distinguished from other kinds of communication – operatively speaking, world political communication then takes place exclusively within,

---

1 Most theories of and in IR are not systems theories in any narrow sense of the term. As a rule, they also do not, or only loosely, refer to systems theories. If used, the term 'system' frequently remains little (or not) specified, is defined as a 'level' of social reality (or analysis), and, often closely linked to the latter point, defined as something emerging out of the interaction of 'units'. The most notable exception to this basic, if possibly somewhat caricatured, understanding of 'systems' in IR were uses and adaptations of cybernetic systems theory for analysing world politics, notably in, and following the work of, Karl Deutsch (see, for example, Deutsch 1966; Baecker 2021 for an overview of systems theories).

and constitutes, such a system of world politics. The system of world politics, in other words, also expresses the internal functional differentiation of the political system (into a range of political fields, ranging from health to education, expressed organizationally in the functional differentiation of government bureaucracies).[2] It also marks the point where evolutionary trajectories with far longer histories, such as diplomacy, all of a sudden find themselves included in a social system that they constitute.

Before elaborating further on what it means to talk about the evolution of a system of world politics, which probably led to systemic differentiation/emergence only around the beginning of the nineteenth century (the Congress of Vienna), it is worth noting that such an evolutionary account of the emergence of a 'system' of modern international/world politics can also be found in places that could not be further removed from explicitly referring to theories of social evolution. Nonetheless, it is perfectly possible to say that at least an implicit social evolutionary understanding is part of IR's most established canon of theorizing about its realm, in this case the struc-

---

2   World politics for quite a while appeared as 'exceptional' in relation to other functionally differentiated subsystems of the political system, as, in addition to a specific symbolically generalized medium of communication (i.e. power observed through the figure of balance), it also operates with a combined 'internal/external' coding and a narrative of structural 'levels' built on that coding: all policy fields are 'internal', everything else is classified under 'external' relations that, taken together, constitute a different 'level' of international politics/an 'international system'. It is only against the powerful semantic structuring effect of that narrative that it can then appear to be a 'novelty' to discover that at some point 'foreign affairs' are no longer the sole prerogative of foreign ministries, but that, for example, ministries of health or education can have 'foreign relations' as well. In fact, it seems that such discoveries actually reproduce the underlying foundational myth that functional differentiation at first happens *within* the segments of a segmented political system (i.e. states), when in fact the functional differentiation of the political system into various realms goes hand in hand with segmentation becoming an important internal differentiation of functionally differentiated subsystems of the political system of world society.

tural realism most notably established through the works of Kenneth Waltz.

Although it does not appear as such on first sight, it is possible to interpret part of Waltz's (1979) celebrated work *Theory of International Politics* as an implicitly evolutionary account, namely his structural-functionalist reading of how the modern states system emerged (see Goddard and Nexon 2005). From contestations between different forms of polity (in terms of social evolution: variations in communications ascribing actorhood to different polities and learning from innovative models), the sovereign state emerged victorious (selection of communications that rationalize the actorhood of states), and on the basis of this selection a system emerged – an 'international system' in Waltz's terms, but also operating under various names, or being included in more general concepts, such as 'international relations', 'international society' or the 'Westphalian system'. In other words: an international system emerged as a social realm in which the restabilization of communications on and by states became the taken-for-granted hegemonic belief. Waltz conceptualizes this analytically as a generative process, where a basic layer produces the next. The basic layer consists of a binary variation of structural form: hierarchical or anarchic, with anarchic being understood as there being no polity that formally rules over the others. The second layer is generated by the condition of anarchy; anarchy means self-help, and self-help means that polities will cope with one another in order to cope with anarchy. The result is that they all end up as sovereign states. This particular form of polity has thus been selected, and others (most notably formal empires and most city-states) have largely been selected out (to survive only in marginalized form as 'city-nation' states, on what still constitutes quite a large spectrum between, for example, Singapore and San Marino). The third layer then models coexistence between these units, which are 'like' (meaning: 'basically similar to') units in constitution, but 'unlike' units in capabilities. The resulting state system is a self-help system where the only difference that counts is the difference in capabilities.

Judged by functional criteria, this construct of Waltz's is an elegantly parsimonious piece of analysis. While attempts at intrinsic critique abound (probably the most elaborate being Buzan, Little and Jones 1993), it seems that there is one line of extrinsic critique that has stuck. This line was inaugurated by Ruggie (1986) and has been expanded and given explicit evolutionary form by Spruyt (1994). Set in the present context, its key point is probably that Waltz's model lies too close to widespread (yet unwarranted) natural evolutionary thinking, and too far away from social evolutionary reasoning. As Spruyt (1994: 5) puts it, the world may be an anarchic place, but it does not follow that units 'operate in a structureless vacuum'. Empirically, in medieval Europe, social relations – differences in trade patterns and class relations – initially spawned not just one, but at least four types of unit: empires, states, city-leagues and city-states. The sovereign state – or more precisely the hegemonic belief in discourses about the centrality of the sovereign state – won out because its standardization programme was more efficient than what the other kinds of unit could deliver (and because the territorial state benefitted from advances in military technology and organization more than the city did).

Autonomization

As mentioned, there is social evolutionary thought, at least of some kind, even in someone who might look like an unusual suspect, namely Kenneth Waltz. It remains largely implicit, but it essentially underpins a story of how something like an 'international system' emerged as a distinct, identifiable and self-identifying social realm. In contrast to structural realism, a 'full' evolutionary account would need to look at the particular selections that led to the emergence of such a system, and especially at the specific ways in which it is distinguished from its environment – here also adopting an understanding of a system that takes it to be constituted by a distinction between system and environment and nothing else (rather than, for example, by 'interacting units'). In this sense, a social evolutionary account will also always be a historical account of the emergence of world politics as a distinct 'system' out of the many structural and semantic traits that will have existed before system evolution ('closure') – without, on the one hand, falling for a 'big bang' historical account (most notably present in the notion of a 'Westphalian system') or, on the other, projecting systemic characteristics backwards onto structurally antecedent forms, thereby constructing historical regularities or even laws that govern how 'international systems' operate throughout history.

In such a reading the systemic quality of world politics is established once a specific type of political communication can clearly be identified as world (or international) politics – and not anything else (or, more precisely, anything else with the same name at the same time). This is an evolutionary process of social differentiation that takes place *within* a political system that includes all political communication, although historically it coevolved with an ongoing functional differentiation of society in which the political system became more clearly differentiated from, for example, an economic system, a system of religion, etc. What is important to note in this respect is that, as a subsystem (or 'part') of the political system, the system of world politics utilizes the same symbolically generalized medium of communication specific to, and constitutive of, the political system, namely power.[3] What makes the system of world politics special and distinct from other functionally differentiated

---

3   This section contains a concise re-presentation and slight further development of the argument put forward in Albert 2016. That argument, like the one presented in this book, is admittedly quite counterintuitive to what could be termed the underlying 'standard' methodologically nationalist view of IR where world/international politics is something that emerges on a level 'above' the political system that is attached firmly to the territorial state. From a world society perspective however, it works exactly the other way around: as functional differentiation becomes more important for, and indeed constitutes, a world society 'level', territorial statehood increasingly functions as one expression among many (see the subsection on hierarchical complexity below) of the *internal* differentiation of a political system of world society – in this case a social differentiation in the form of *segmentation*. On the heuristic usefulness of the concept of symbolically generalized media of communication (originally taken from Parsons and developed much further in the context of a theory of social systems by Luhmann) in IR, see, recently, Peña and Davies 2022.

subsystems of the political system is its use of a specific 'program' for observing and processing that symbolically generalized medium of communication, namely the figure of the 'balance of power'. 'Balance of power' becomes the basic scheme through which world politics is observed: this does not mean that balance of power politics covers everything, or that a Newtonian balancing of forces within a system would constitute some kind of 'natural' law. Quite the contrary. 'Balance of power', as an observational scheme, often operates in the background. This is not akin to claiming that all world politics would be balance of power politics, or that 'interest defined as power' (Morgenthau) would always take precedence over norms-based policies in the context of a balance of power system. It is, however, to highlight why a 'realist' worldview of this kind possesses so much intuitive appeal, since it claims that the most relevant political practices are those that are most similar in form to that observational scheme (see also Müller and Albert 2021). To put it differently: there is little doubt that the balance of power(s) is not a recent invention of 'modern' world politics. With its Western ideational roots most strongly anchored in the Investiture Controversy, and its modern epistemological and ontological expression most visible in a Newtonian worldview, it can be said with virtual certainty that the heyday of explicit balancing politics, rooted in and accompanied by a vast balance of power literature, lay in the eighteenth rather than the nineteenth century. What happened at the turn of that century, however, crystallizing in the Congress of Vienna, was a formalization of the balance of power principle that, in an important sense, relieved individual powers of always having to construct a 'balancing world' of their own, so to speak. 'Balance of power' turned from a principle that required constant individual actualization to an observational scheme characteristic of, and thereby also constitutively underlying the formation of, a distinct system, which, as a result of that scheme, differentiated itself from its environment. By analogy with the modern world of computing, from being a multiplicity of programs/applications balance of power turned into an operating system: all programs run on it, though this also means that not everything runs directly at the operating system level.

This autonomization of a system of world politics highlights the fact that autonomization and (hierarchical) complexity are deeply interwoven: social evolutionary analysis does not stop at the variation and selection of communications about hegemonic forms of organizing political authority (as nation-state, city-state, etc.) within a given social realm. It also highlights the historical formation of the resulting realm itself as a distinct level of social reality. In this sense, the formation of modern world politics is not only characterized by evolutionary experiments with fundamentally different forms of organizing political authority, such as empires vs nation-states or the plurality of different communities of practice. Rather, there are also important evolutionary advances, which make world politics distinguishable as a distinct level of social reality by giving it its specific medium and form, in this case the 'balance of power'. The Congress of Vienna in this sense could be described as an evolutionary tipping point underpinning the establishment of the 'balance of power' as the main discursive formation through which world politics describes and observes itself. It was preceded by a long history of experimenting with different discursive attempts at solving the problem of how sovereigns, that by definition (and particularly if sovereignty is seen to derive from God) are above everyone and everything else, can relate to one another on equal terms and thereby constitute the realm of the 'international' in social practice (Kuntz 2018). After the selection of discursive formations converging around notions of the balance of power as a formal organizing principle after the Napoleonic wars, restabilization – and the forms of vertical power legitimized on that basis – became evident by the consolidation of a range of important systemic innovations that thereafter facilitated communications in world politics, most importantly the formalization and routinization of diplomatic protocol through the Congress System.

Hierarchical complexity

As Spruyt reminds us, this evolution of modern world politics did not take place in a social vacuum. Politics coevolves with other systems such as the legal one, though not in perfect synchronicity (Brunkhorst 2014). More generally, modern (world) society sets boundary conditions for what can be selected, and what cannot, in distinct (sub)systems or social realms, and supports restabilizations in such contexts. To put it directly, in a situation where the French Revolution symbolized the demise of an order of society that was primarily characterized by stratification and possessed a clear order of social classes, it was highly improbable that classical empires, which epitomized stratification on a global scale, could survive in the long run. Throughout the nineteenth and early twentieth centuries, the classical empire became increasingly contested and was ultimately deselected as a form of organizing political authority in world politics (leaving behind 'informal empires' such as the USSR or the US). We do not aim at this stage to embark further on the evolution of the modern (nation-)state system. The point here is not to focus on the immense variety of variations, selections, and restabilizations in this system within and between different communities of practice (as in the debates on a post-Westphalian or post-colonial order, the rise of international organizations, different security imperatives etc.). From our point of view, it is clear that the evolution of world politics never comes to a standstill as long as system-internal communications and contestations – the carriers of evolution – endure and link up to one another by being observed, within this social realm, as decisive for the distribution ('balance') of power. Contra Tang (2013), world politics is built on change, not stasis, and this includes change on the level of its basic operating principles and its constitutive forms of actorhood. It definitely includes more dimensions than 'anarchy' or 'empire' and is about much more than a movement between statist notions of offensive vs defensive realism, as Tang holds. It always experiments with variations and, through endless chains of communications, (un)selects different forms of organizing political authority, including the actors (among them, communities of practice) that embody these forms.

It is at this point that the evolution *of* the system ties up with evolution *within* the system. Reconstructing the trajectory of social evolution from a contemporary perspective, the sovereign territorial nation-state becomes the primary dominant form of organizing political authority in the system of world politics. However, and particularly also aided by the normative stabilization of the system of international law (see below), this primacy *never* completely displaces other forms, but arranges them in a hierarchical complexity with the nation-state at the 'top', so to speak. While, most notably, formal empires become delegitimized, imperiality as a form of organizing political authority persists (Schlichte and Stetter 2023).[4] Both mainly state-based global governance arrangements and forms of 'private' authority are incorporated into an overall system of world politics. It is important to note that, while, of course, there is competition between different forms of organizing political authority – including potential challenges for the 'top place' in the system – there is no zero-sum game involved here. Just as, historically, imperial-colonial and nation-state-building projects competed with, but also mutually reinforced, one another, so forms of 'public' and 'private' authority both compete with and reinforce each other too.[5] The system of world politics evolves as an ever-changing agglomeration of forms of organizing political authority in a relation of hierarchical complexity. That specific forms completely disappear or completely new ones appear seems to be the exception; rearrangements under the condition of hierarchical complexity seems to be the rule.

The restabilization of world politics and its coevolution with (international) law

The evolution of even the, relatively speaking, most autonomous social systems does not take place in a social vacuum. Social systems coevolve, often being more strongly linked to some social systems rather than others. Law and politics, with their emergent internal differentiation and the formation of systems of international law and world politics, are, arguably, the two most closely coupled systems.[6]

---

4 See Mackenzie 2016 for what is probably the best definition of empire across the variety of forms of empire in world history.

5 In the parlance of the so-called 'English School' of International Relations (ES), this hints at the mutual constitution and reinforcement of 'world society' and 'international society' (in the ES understanding of the terms); see e.g. Bucher and Eckl 2021.

6 See again Brunkhorst 2014 for a comprehensive account in terms of social evolution; Albert 2002 for an account in non-evolutionary terms.

It should be noted in this respect, however, that a close linkage to each other is not an argument against the diagnosis of systemic autonomy as a result of functional differentiation. Quite the contrary. It is only as a result of functional differentiation that different systems can be observed and described as distinct from one another, which, in turn, allows strong links to emerge (although these links themselves need not appear out of the blue, but can continue previous historical pathways of evolution). The legal system sets normative conditions for the likelihood of selections in the political system (and vice versa), although it does not strictly condition them.

It is in this sense that it is possible to say that, while the social evolution of stratified societies was characterized by an ongoing systemic (functional) differentiation of law and politics, operating together the two formed one single complex of social integration, both likewise in close conjunction with religious worldviews. This social complex was closely related to the restabilization of the societal structure of socially differentiated classes and politically centralized empires. The tremendous growth of communicative negations and, thereby, the potential variation triggered by the intellectual (e.g. by prophets, scribes, teachers and philosophers) and administrative uses of scripture was, however, neutralized by the socially selective integration of all preadaptive advances. This happened through the academic organization of philosophical discourses, the clerical organization of religious transcendence, as well as the cosmopolitan multiculturalism and legal universalism that developed ever new means of restabilizing the existing structure of political class-rule. Thus, autonomization slowly emerged not only within the political but also within the religious and legal spheres. However, preadaptive advances in normative universalism and functional differentiation that have been observed since the eleventh century ultimately paved the way for a coevolution of religious-legal rationalism and autonomous political power. This process also triggered a dialectic between a (real) polis and an (imagined) cosmopolis in this coevolution of law and politics. In particular, this dialectic was functionally needed for imperial coordination (through Roman Civil Law) and the ideological justification (through theories of the sovereign) of class-rule. Yet, it also articulated the normative tension between religious promises of egalitarian justice and salvation, on the one hand, and the undeserved suffering, exploitation and enslavement of the lower social strata of society, on the other – thus unintentionally giving rise to previously inconceivable discursive negations that gave rise in turn to religious (e.g. the Reformation) and political (e.g. the French Revolution) upheavals.

For the coevolution of law and politics (as two autonomous spheres) – as well as of a (primarily) politically defined particularism and a (primarily) legally and religiously defined cosmopolitanism – the Papal Legal Revolution of the eleventh and twelfth centuries was the tipping point (Berman 1985; Brunkhorst 2014). In Western Europe, it triggered the functional differentiation of law, and, as a result, that of religion and (higher) education too. It (unintentionally) separated the sacred and profane spheres of value. It translated into the differentiation between city-states, city leagues, monarchies, the Holy Roman Empire and the cosmopolitan Church state. This coevolution of law and politics and, in conjunction, the ideas of universal and particular statehood then turned into something like a guiding paradigm for the Western legal tradition. In particular, it led to several preadaptive advances in modern constitutional law, that is, early forms of structural coupling between law and politics, on the one hand, and of the dialectic between universal and particular rights and legal principles (i.e. normative constraints), on the other.

One key element here was the replacement in all diplomatic affairs of cousins, uncles, brothers and all other kins- and tribesmen by professional lawyers after the Peace of Westphalia and, in particular, from the Congress of Vienna on. This was the first great step in realizing an autonomous sphere of trans-urban, trans-monarchical, trans-imperial and, ultimately, international relations (Fried 1974). Since the great legal revolution of the eleventh and twelfth centuries, diplomacy thus gradually became a privilege of lawyers. The juridification of war set in. And the alternative between waging war and searching for judicial dispute settlement was established (ibid.; see also the illustrative case of global peacebuilding discussed below). Moreover, the dialectic of the national and the cosmopolitan legal/political order was restabilized again and again after every great revolution. The paradigm of the national state is thus under pressure from two historical ends. Contemporary world society is not shaped merely by the effects of global problems. These problems are now widely perceived and defined as the common problems of mankind, and this is possible only because world society is already, at least partly, a normatively integrated society. Taking both ends of the history of the modern state together, one could argue for a paradigm shift in the theory of the modern state and state-based international relations. The national state is a borderline case of statehood, a very specific historical case that is not at all the perfect form of *the* state or the telos and essence of 3,000 years of state evolution.

On the global level there exists today a *res publica* constituted by public law and public affairs, which affects all world citizens and is widely recognized (von Bogdandy 2012). This modern legal/political order is in this respect not unlike the old Roman order or the medieval Church State – it is a republic without a (territorial/national) state. But this global republic, consisting of networks of inter-, trans- and supranational organizations, realizes a kind of statehood because it increasingly not only supplements state functions but substitutes for them (Albert 2005: 229). To say that some form of world statehood actually does exist may sound quite strange: however, it only does so if world statehood is equated with the idea of exclusive statehood associated with the doctrine of sovereign territorial statehood. Embedded in a systemic environment characterized by hierarchical complexity, it is only one form of organizing political authority next to, and in addition to, others (see Albert et al. 2008).

4.2 The restabilization of world politics and peacebuilding

As we outlined in the previous section, a process of autonomization of the realm of world politics and a (relative) hegemony of balance of power as the underpinning organizing 'program' within it characterize world politics in the contemporary era. Its autonomization has two main facets: a differentiation from other social realms, on the one hand, and internal differentiation, on the other. The former is visible in the evolution of operational logics unique to world politics (and not found in other social realms), first and foremost the organizing principle of balance of power; the latter can be studied by looking at the emergence and consolidation of distinct 'institutional complexes' (defined by specific social structures, practices, actor constellations and semantics) within the system of world politics. This is what we will be looking at in this section, studying the emergence and consolidation of 'peacebuilding' as such an institutional complex. As a reminder, both external and internal differentiation are processes triggered by variations – based, as we have detailed above, on strategic or accidental contestations and the spread of new ideas. Variations are, of course, ubiquitous occurrences in the social world. Only some lead to meaningful selections that take root, thereby becoming consolidated as new social practices. If this happens, these practices can ultimately contribute to a restabilization of a given social realm expressed both in terms of its becoming distinguishable from other realms (the social and non-social environments) and in the form of ongoing internal differentiation. That is why we can talk of autonomization of *and* within a system.

However, differentiation within a system, the topic that we are studying in this section, is not a linear affair. One should not assume ever increasing internal differentiation that would, over time, amount to complete fragmentation. In evolutionary processes some forms of internal differentiation emerge, while others wither away or change fundamentally. Think here of the distinction between civilized and non-civilized peoples based on racial differentiation in world politics – the so-called 'standard of civilization' – which was a guiding normative principle in the nineteenth and early twentieth century, underpinned by a widely shared ideology of 'scientific racism' (Buzan and Lawson 2015; Hobson 2012). Over time, though, the 'standard of civilization' became widely delegitimized in the context of genocides and other grave crimes against humanity committed by Western nations, as well as by the advance of decolonization and the development of the UN system. Thus, while some principles, like the 'standard of civilization', fade away (or at least are fundamentally transformed, see Buzan 2014), new forms of internal differentiation can emerge. This is what we will look at in this section by studying the emergence of discourses and practices of peacebuilding as one form of internal differentiation in world politics. We refer to peacebuilding in relation to the semantics, practices, actor constellations and structures that are deployed, either globally or in regional theatres, in order to contain violence and, through international rather than unilateral interventions, underpin internationally embedded regimes of peace in designated 'conflict zones'. Peacebuilding is, thus, understood here as a densely institutionalized complex within the system of world politics, a fundamental building block of its constitutional structure (cf. Reus-Smit 1999).

Our argument about 'internal differentiation' thus bears some resemblance to those concepts in IR that study the consolidation of core practice fields and normative ideas in world politics, such as the concept of primary institutions (Buzan 2004), which captures some of the basic ideas of internal differentiation well. Thus, core primary institutions – Buzan, for example, mentions sovereignty, diplomacy, territoriality, great power management, market governance, nationalism, human rights, environmental stewardship and others (ibid.) – are, on the one hand, specific to world politics (i.e. attest to external differentiation), while, on the other, making up this system's complex internal differentiation. Since they go hand in hand with notions of legitimate action, legitimized actorhood (cf. Meyer and Jepperson 2000; Manning 1962) and forms of bureaucratic organization, primary institutions are quite similar to what we referred to above as institutional complexes. However, Buzan omits peacebuilding, at least as a primary institution, only mentioning peacekeeping operations as a so-called secondary institution. Yet, given the rich literature in peace and conflict studies that attests to the extensive organizational and normative anchoring of peacebuilding in world politics, we consider it a far more central building block of world politics, very much in line with what primary institutions are about.

Institutionalized complexes are not static. While some endure, new selections may transform or even replace antecedents. That is why a general trend towards entropy, in other words, a relative growth of different institutionalized complexes within a given system can be expected. World politics is no exception here, as the literature on primary institutions underlines, with their number arguably having grown over time. The simultaneity of different institutionalized complexes within a social realm can foster 'contradictions' or seeming paradoxes, for instance when we observe a growing centrality of both sovereignty (e.g. through decolonization and the expansion of international society) and external interventions in erstwhile sacrosanct prerogatives of state sovereignty (e.g. based on the consolidation of peacebuilding as a highly legitimized field of action) at the same time. Or think of the rise of nationalism and self-determination, which can lead both to a neat consolidation of territories under nation-state rule bordering each other and also to offensive claims on other people's territory. Where such tensions exist, they tend, from the perspective of the overall system, to attest to an increasing consolidation of the system's external differentiation, since they are largely based on internal dynamics – such as struggles within and across primary institutions with respect to their specific outlook – that clearly distinguish the system in question, say world politics, from others. This confirms Luhmann's observation that systems are characterized by differentiation rather than unity and homogeneity, world politics being no exception in that respect.

In precisely this way peacebuilding can be understood as contributing to the autonomization of world politics. As part of the internal differentiation of world politics, over the course of at least the last two centuries, peacebuilding has become a densely institutionalized complex within it. Some violent conflicts, but not all (more on that below), are seen as relevant to its overall system, requiring international interventions in the form of peacebuilding to curtail violence in conflict zones and establish 'peace'. As we explain below, such interventions revolve around the evolution of an ideal of non-violence that has, over time, become firmly anchored in world politics diplomatically, legally and normatively (Linklater 2016). This ideal should not be understood in an idealistic way, however, but in its relationship with the underpinning 'program' of world politics, namely its relation to the maintenance, or transformation, of the actual balance of power predominating in a given era.

This embedding of peacebuilding within the paradigm of the balance of power is particularly apparent on two levels. Firstly, and as far as autonomization is concerned, it is to be found in the overarching securitization logic of world politics reflected in the notion of 'zones of peace' and 'zones of war', both globally and regionally (see Buzan and Wæver 2005), to which peacebuilding is tightly linked. In fact, as Article 1.1 of the UN Charter elaborates, 'peace' and 'security' are regarded as two sides of the same coin. Secondly, it is evident when one addresses hierarchical complexity, as we do below, building on Richmond's (2006) genealogy of peacebuilding. Thus, we can identify several stages in the evolution of peacebuilding that closely correspond with a given form of, or disputes regarding, the balance of power dominant in world politics in different eras. Prevailing notions of 'peace' in world politics – including alternative concepts – have never been insulated from claims to authority (*Herrschaft*): from the reactionary forms of the victor's peace hegemonic throughout most of the nineteenth century to the emancipatory forms of peacebuilding aimed at transforming a merely state-based balance of power, which have been on the rise since at least the 1960s and highlight human security, local security and positive peace thereby challenging statism, Eurocentrism and great power interests (Autesserre 2009).

But before we study the peculiarities of peacebuilding as an institutionalized complex we have to first ask the basic sociological question as to why violent conflicts have become an object of observation in world politics in the first place. A short detour into conflict theory is useful here, for it will allow us to discuss the challenge that conflicts, in particular violent conflicts, pose for any system.

As conflict theories from Georg Simmel to Louis Coser, Niklas Luhmann and Heinz Messmer have shown, conflict is a social structure that has its own in-built inclination to escalate and colonize or even destroy its 'host system'. A complete overarching of world politics by violent conflicts would threaten system stability, in the form of total war, Armageddon or some other doomsday scenario. One might also think here of spatial contexts in which violence rules (almost) unconstrained and, as a result, violence rather than power (i.e. social relationships in which at least some form of political legitimacy is sought) shapes social relations, as for example in Nazi extermination camps or gang- and militia-ridden favelas in deprived neighbourhoods across Central and Latin America.

The in-built tendency of social conflicts to escalate is the reason why the institutionalization of practices aiming to contain conflicts is not unique to the (world) political system, but can be observed in various social realms. More specifically, in the context of functional differentiation different systems have developed their own distinct forms of regulating conflicts and the modern era is characterized by a widely positively-connotated impulse to actively address and name such conflicts, while engaging in their resolution in a professionalized (and highly individualized) manner that aims to establish 'peaceful relations': from constitutions that define the parameters of political conflict resolution in mainly national political systems to positive law that can be evoked in courts, and from mediation at the workplace and in families to psychotherapy, the latter addressing inner conflicts, with therapists acting as 'peacebuilders'. Seen from that perspective, it becomes clear why, within the political system, only a certain amount of violent conflict can be tolerated, such as – as far as world politics is concerned – in the provisions of the UN charter, which in Chapter VII limits the use of physical violence to national or collective self-defence against aggression or UN Security Council-mandated military interventions to 'maintain or restore international peace and security'. But what does the 'international' in international peace and security refer to? This is precisely about the politics of peacebuilding, the evolution of semantics and practices that determine which violent conflicts count as targets of international intervention.

In that sense, (violent) conflicts contribute to the evolution of world politics. This is very much in line with a general function of conflicts, namely to prevent stasis in a system, which is well reflected in the psychological notion of 'not suppressing' conflicts. The challenge for any system then, including politics, is to integrate conflicts within the overall system logic and its main programmes, allowing them to trigger evolutionary adaptation. Historically, one can think here of the way in which the (violent) conflicts over decolonization revealed, in Europe and elsewhere, that there are polities beyond the imperial powers with claims to political (self-)determination. Under that premise conflicts can be a resource for learning and flexibility, although there is always the possibility of escalation that could disrupt a system or threaten its very existence. There is, thus, a thin line between giving space to (and even encouraging) conflicts, on the one hand, and avoiding their unrestrained escalation, on the other. There is also an evolutionary component to this because conflicts as sites of contestation – defined by the repeated communication of a 'no' (Stetter 2014) – are closely linked to variation, a prerequisite for any adaptation to changing environments. This can be observed in political theory as well, for example in Chantal Mouffe's (1999) theory of agonistic conflicts, in which she argues that even stark conflicts of identity should be moved into the centre of political struggles, and that this will ultimately contribute to (democratic) stability. Bahar Rumelili and Lisa Strömbom (2022: 4) have put forward a similar argument in relation to 'agonistic peacebuilding', suggesting that preserving a sense of 'ontological security' among conflicting parties in international politics will, in certain contexts, require stopping short of a complete transformation of conflicting identities in order to avoid a backlash that would only harden those identities. Thus, 'the continuity and stability of self-narratives and the ideological and moral certainty provided by the conflict's "formed framework"' (ibid.) must, through statecraft and everyday politics, be balanced with the gradual establishment of political structures that overcome inimical Self/Other distinctions. In short, any social realm is confronted with the challenge of seeking a balance between allowing and containing conflicts – or, in evolutionary terms, finding an answer to the question of how much contestation and conflict is bearable for further evolution.

All this is, finally, complicated by the fact that, given the ubiquity of conflicts, including violent conflicts, in the social world, it cannot be determined ex ante which of these (violent) conflicts are to be seen as politically relevant within the realm of world politics. To resort to the terminology of securitization theory, the evolution of peacebuilding can thus be understood as an ever ongoing political struggle over which referent objects are legitimate targets of political measures (e.g. international/regional peace and stability, state sovereignty, independence, human rights, local peace, etc.), the definition of 'existential threats' (e.g. those of a transborder nature, 'domestic' conflicts or even 'structural' root causes such as climate change or poverty, etc.) and the security professionals that should be involved in peacebuilding (state leaders, diplomats, IOs, developmental assistance personnel, NGOs staff, local communities, etc.). Overall, such political struggles over what counts as an 'international' conflict requiring action at the level of world politics are a defining feature of the evolution, and conceptual widening, of peacebuilding witnessed over the course of the last 200 years – revolving, as we will discuss in more detail below, around the ideal of non-violence that underpins peacebuilding, on the one hand, and being closely linked to either the maintenance/defence of hegemonic manifestations of the balance of power or resistance to them and their transformation as the underlying 'programme' of world politics, on the other.

Autonomization

The selection of discourses and practices related to an emergent ideal of non-violence – which, admittedly, is regularly evoked in order to justify the use of violence, as in so-called humanitarian interventions or on the basis of claims of resistance – has contributed to the consolidation of a distinct institutional complex within the system of world politics, thereby attesting to the overall process of internal differentiation. In accordance with a broad strand of literature in peace and conflict studies we identify this institutional complex as the realm of 'peacebuilding'. We transcend this literature, however, by highlighting in what follows the systematic embedding of peacebuilding within an overall logic of the autonomization of world politics. Core to our argument is that there has been a process of social and cognitive (normative) learning in world politics – revolving around a hegemonic ideal of non-violence (see Koloma Beck and Werron 2017) – that underpins the consolidation of peacebuilding as a specific form of internal differentiation within the realm of world politics. Two interrelated dynamics stand out here. Firstly, the emergence and subsequent consolidation of semantics and practices in world politics that not only allow instances of violence to be regarded as a challenge to international peace and security that has to be addressed by (international) peacebuilding, but links this to an ideal of non-violence that structures this institutional complex. Secondly, an increasing (hierarchical) complexity within this institutional complex. From the nineteenth century until today we have witnessed constant change in what peacebuilding is about, with 'older' versions, such as the victor's peace, transforming but not disappearing, and many newer forms, such as 'institutional peace' or 'emancipatory peace' (see Richmond 2006) enriching the arsenal of peacebuilding semantics and practices. In that context the link between the practice of peacebuilding and the way peace is studied academically deserves attention too, for example the growing emphasis on 'structural peace' and 'positive peace' (Galtung 1969; Senghaas 1982) or the more recent 'local turn' (MacGinty and Richmond 2013). Central here is the observation that notwithstanding an increasing autonomization of peacebuilding within the system of world politics, both the prevalent practices and the alternative/critical approaches remain closely linked to the overall 'programme' of balance of power – either in an affirmative way (the bulk of liberal peacebuilding practices) or *ex negativo*, by actively challenging prevailing state-based, Western forms of balance of power in critical peacebuilding practices.

This underlying linkage and hierarchy between balance of power, on the one hand, and peacebuilding, on the other, figures in the fundamental division into 'two worlds' (Buzan and Wæver 2005: 125) that shapes international security architectures and conflict formations. This has to do with the question of which conflicts and which world regions are regularly addressed in world political arenas as threats to security and as sites of intervention. As Oliver Richmond (2006) explains, a major selection made here is the social construction of a zone of conflict, identified with the Global South as a realm of insecurities and as an object of interventions, vis-à-vis a zone of peace, associated with the Global North, in particular the Atlantic–Pacific West, but also comprising other regions and states that follow the West's model of security, especially by setting up regional security communities, such as ASEAN or the AU. Furthermore, this 'zone of peace' – jointly with International Organizations and NGOs – is the major provider of international security in the form of interventions by military, developmental, economic, cultural and diplomatic means. There is, in other words, an underlying distribution of power and hierarchy when it comes to peacebuilding and the fundamental distinction between zones of peace and zones of conflict is itself an expression of an underlying balance of power principle governing world politics. While we share with critical approaches in peace and conflict studies and IR the view that many postcolonial injustices and Orientalist tropes are connected to this notion of 'a zone of peace and a zone of conflict' (Buzan and Wæver 2005: 18), our evolutionary approach allows us to theorize the reasons related to the rise and persistence of this binary structure. Thus, because peacebuilding does not constitute a completely autonomous realm of world society in its own right, its semantics and practices are linked to the maintenance or challenging of concrete manifestations of 'balance of power', whether in the distinction between UN veto power countries and other states, the West and the rest or the aforementioned 'zones of peace' and 'zones of conflict'. This, to be sure, is relevant not only to debates on peacebuilding. It is also of concern to many mainstream liberal, social constructivist, institutionalist and realist IR theories that either ignore balance of power altogether – presumably because of this concept's 'realist' odour (liberalism, institutionalism, social constructivism) or because hierarchies are neglected on the basis of ahistorical (and Eurocentric) assumptions about anarchy (various brands of realism and geopolitics, but also Wendtian US-constructivism).

This embedding of peacebuilding within the 'balance of power' logic of world politics systematically structures semantics and practices of peacebuilding. While the ideal of non-violence allows us, in theory (see below), to identify all possible forms of (political) violence as legitimate targets of peacebuilding, this is filtered by the balance of power principle. Thus, violent political conflicts within the territory of states with UN veto power or linked to such states (as in the case of China's Xinjang province, Russia's war against Ukraine since 2014/2022, the fabricated arguments for the US intervention in Iraq 2003, etc.) are usually not subject to peacebuilding, or only in their aftermaths (as in Iraq) – although normatively these conflict sites are widely seen by global publics, NGOs and even a UN special rapporteur in the case of the Uyghurs as threats to security and gross violations of human rights. Consequently, the bulk of UN peacebuilding, following a similar balance of power logic, has been aimed at conflict sites beyond the 'zones of peace' – to various locations in the (extended) Global South, Timor-Leste, Cambodia, the Congo, Lebanon and Cyprus, rather than to the mainly Western core, think of the Basque Country, South Tyrol and Northern Ireland.

Overall, prevailing notions of peace – and challenges to them – are closely related to historically hegemonic manifestations of the balance of power, that are either defended or challenged, but in either case provide the underlying foundation of peacebuilding. This was already the case with the hyper-conservative (Richmond 2006) notions of international peace that emerged during the nineteenth century, defined the maintenance of peace and security as the 'white man's burden', and problematized 'local violence' while legitimizing imperial counterinsurgency. Of course, hyper-conservative notions did not remain uncontested, they were challenged by leaders, civil society actors (including in the West, e.g. philanthropic societies) and non-Western elites – and it is precisely these variations in the form of contestations that explain the gradual differentiation of new semantics and practices of peacebuilding. While the balance of power principle has been with us since at least the Congress of Vienna in 1815, its specific outlook has changed. And so has the outlook of peacebuilding. The specific semantics and practices of constraining, managing and rationalizing organized political violence for the sake of (international) 'peace' have altered considerably over time. That is why the history of organized violence in world politics can be read not only as the evolution of wars, old and new (Kaldor 1999; Bartelson 2017), but also as the history of the manifold ways of managing these conflicts and bringing about 'peace'. The emergence since the nineteenth century of an institutional complex of peacebuilding attests, in sum, to two dynamics. Firstly, the restabilization of peacebuilding as an institutional complex within the realm of world politics, triggered by variations in the nature of violent conflicts that have led to the selection of new ideas for regulating these conflicts by, say, congress diplomacy, global multilateral institutions, international law (coevolution with law, see below) or new normative practices linked to initially marginalized conceptions of a shared humanity that gradually replaced various forms of (scientific) racism as the legitimate view of humankind as a whole (coevolution with normative consciousness, see also below). Secondly, this institutional 'thickening' of peacebuilding, in particular when seen in conjunction with the thickening of other internally differentiated realms of world politics (say, primary institutions such as trade, diplomacy, war, environmental politics, human rights regimes, etc.) and the joint linkage of these realms to the underpinning principle of balance of power stabilizes the autonomization of world politics as a system.

Key to understanding peacebuilding in the modern international system, then, is the notion that observing violent conflicts not only legitimizes the use of violence through various practices related to the evolution of war (self-defence, having recourse to legitimizing programmes based on sovereignty, nationalism and suchlike, protection of global/regional security mandated by the UN Charter etc.) but also defines conflict as something that needs to be actively contained by means of peacebuilding. While it can reasonably be argued that the sites of violence that are observed as potentially relevant to 'international peace and security' have expanded over the course of the last two centuries, still only a tiny number of (violent) conflicts are considered as relevant to world politics. Thus, bullying involving 16-year-old girls and boys in a schoolyard in Jakarta or Geneva is unlikely to be elevated to the status of a political problem that triggers variations and selections in world politics – but it might be at the national level, giving rise, for example, to new educational programmes, penal laws, etc. By contrast, since the nineteenth century violence between social groups, particularly between those that define themselves on the basis of ethno-national belonging and are pursuing self-determination (resulting in inter-state wars, civil wars, decolonization, etc.), has regularly been framed as related to international peace and security – and regularly becomes subject to peacebuilding endeavours. From the perspective of a theory of evolution, this sensitivity of world politics (and other social realms, such as mass media, academia, law, education, etc.) to violent conflicts is not a given, but itself subject to social evolution

– and not only because, prior to the nineteenth century, no norm of 'nationalism' existed on the basis of which communications could be clustered in a discursive formation based on self-determination and conflicts related to it. The same is true for human rights violations and how they trigger conflicts. In addition, this can only be seen as threatening international peace and security if at least some form of human rights regime has emerged, either in positive law, political practice or from various human rights' advocates. A set-up in which (violent) conflicts are a case for (international) peacebuilding is thus a major site for political struggles. Over the course of the last two centuries these struggles have led to considerable changes in the definition of what constitutes a conflict and what are legitimate forms of peacebuilding. If violent conflicts are addressed on that basis, they trigger variations in the system of world politics and lead eventually to selections that establish peacebuilding as a major site, or institutional complex, of world politics.

The ideal of non-violence plays a major role in this context, for it provides the semantic and practical background for viewing 'violence' as something that ought to be opposed in the name of security and peace, even if this includes temporarily enacting violence for the sake of 'international peace' (e.g. robust mandates given to UN peacekeepers, humanitarian interventions). Koloma Beck and Werron (2017) have shown how the discursive frame of 'local' violence as a world political problem emerged in the course of the nineteenth century, and how this fostered a 'hegemonic ideal' of non-violence in international politics, the ideational underpinning of the peace-building paradigm. On that basis, semantics and practices related to this ideal stabilized, including a wide variety of communities of practice that at least partly legitimized their actorhood in relation to this ideal (e.g. great powers, International Organizations and non-governmental organizations). While the question as to which forms of 'local' violence are regarded as a world political problem – in other words the politics of peacebuilding – remains deeply contested until today (Autesserre 2009), regarding selected instances of local violence as issues that need to be solved in world politics based on an ideal of non-violence has had tremendous effects. Koloma Beck and Werron (2017: 279) highlight in that context a 'progressive delegalization and delegitimation' of inter- and intra-state violence. This should not, though, be misread as 'straightforwardly progressive' (ibid.) not least because the ideal of non-violence 'embeds local conflicts into global competitions' (ibid. 286). These competitions can result in a given conflict becoming the object of peacebuilding but can also, paradoxically, trigger violence. An example would be where conflict parties aim to draw attention to 'their' conflict or subtly induce their enemies to use violence in order to increase global attention. Moreover, as mentioned above, observing violence through the prism of the ideal of non-violence shapes semantic disguises of the use of violence, such as in humanitarian interventions.

The evolution of this ideal of non-violence was initially based on isolated variations to the 'normal' way of doing things by great powers, in other words it was about contestations that challenged the practice of great power politics in dependent territories. The ideal of non-violence is closely related to the 'human rights revolution' (Akira et al. 2012) that emerged in world politics around the same time Since the late eighteenth century claims for self-determination from Haiti to Greece – and supported by social movements 'which campaigned against specific forms of cruelty or violence which were not yet regulated by national jurisdiction' (Koloma Beck and Werron 2017: 277) linked the ideal of non-violence (which required temporary resistance to colonialism though) with the human rights of every individual, including self-determination for non-Westerners, as an alternative to the entrenched state-centred, colonial and imperial practices that dominated world politics in that epoch (see Reus-Smit 2001). In sum, the 'de-legalization of inter-state violence was to be closely interlinked with the codification of human rights' (ibid.: 278). Over time, these more or less isolated communicative variations paved the way for selections that translated these variations into the aforementioned discourses, practices, forms of knowledge and models of actorhood that started to shape the newly emerging institutional complex of (international) peacebuilding. Initially (see also below), great powers tried to accommodate these novel semantics within their entrenched power prerogatives (e.g. by jointly administering parts of China and the Ottoman Empire), but in that era other forms of peacebuilding were already emerging that attested to an evolution in this institutional complex itself.

This internal differentiation of world politics, indicative of a process of autonomization, is a perspective on international politics that Tang (2013), for example, completely misses in his state-centric evolutionist ontology.[7] What he observes is merely a shift to a defensive realist world, a rather simplistic concept in light of the multiplicity of quasi-constitutional structures in world politics anyway. What he overlooks is the immense institutional density and complexity of world politics, a field that comprises a much broader set of constitutional structures than realist orthodoxy allows, and of which peacebuilding revolving around an ideal of non-violence is one element. To sum up, semantics and practices explicitly linked to a hegemonic ideal of non-violence contributed to the internal differentiation of world politics. In theory, and once this ideal has become sufficiently anchored across various communities of practice as well as in people's minds (and in legal frameworks), almost every conflict in which violence occurs – or could potentially occur – can become a theatre of peacebuilding. The question as to which concrete actions and actors are considered legitimate in peacebuilding has evolved – but can be well studied by turning to the hierarchical complexity of peacebuilding, which we examine in the next section on the basis of Richmond's (2006) genealogy.

Hierarchical Complexity

This autonomization of world politics, based on internal differentiation that includes inter alia the stabilization of peacebuilding as one of its core institutional complexes, is not static. Peacebuilding is subject to hierarchical complexity, with the notion of 'liberal peace' (Richmond 2006: 193) becoming a hegemonic, but contested ideal over time. The hierarchical complexity of peacebuilding figures in

---

7   Before the 1990s, peace and reconciliation was often affected by third parties that mediated/created back channels between states. Mediating conflicts inside a sovereign state, however, was exceptional. Nonetheless, since the late 1980s and especially the 1990s, it has become standard: Israel, Guatemala, Sri Lanka, Spain are telling examples (Neumann 2015).

the selection – and at times the deselection – of specific procedures, discourses, practices, institutions, programmes and mentalities intended to ensure peace through collective interventions by the 'international community', thereby containing the uncontrolled spread of violence and establishing some form of legitimate authority that secures 'peace'. The collective interventions through which this took place changed over time. Firstly, there were joint colonial intrusions, for example into China in the nineteenth century or into the Ottoman Empire where a British protectorate was established in Egypt and an Austro-Hungarian protectorate in Bosnia and Herzegovina in spite of the *de iure* sovereignty of the Ottoman Empire to which these territories formally belonged. These were followed, secondly, by trusteeship and great power management before and after World War I, for example under the mandate system. Thirdly came state-building orchestrated by international organizations, or contemporary humanitarian interventions and developmental assistance. In all these settings the question of which conflicts were considered a threat to the system remained paramount – and for that reason the definition of which conflicts should become sites of 'peacebuilding' is still a heavily politicized field. It is, that is to say, a discursive context in which variations occur, some of them selected as viable peacebuilding measures, some not – all of them being closely related to the overarching context of how they affect or change the hegemonic manifestations of the balance of power in a given era. While world politics arguably continues to be read in terms of secure vs insecure spaces, the former associated with the Global North, in particular the West, the latter with the Global South, changes are evident. Thus, the 'zone of peace' has gradually expanded (Richmond 2006: 190) to include today 'dominant actors in International or Regional Environment' (ibid.) such as international and regional organizations and regional powers from the Global South that have become central actors in peacebuilding. This evolution of the notion of zones of peace is mirrored by the evolution of the 'zone of conflict' in which a growing number of issues have been defined as threats to peace, a growing number of institutional programs enacted and, finally, a growing number of actors identified as not only recipients but subjects of peacebuilding (including local communities and individuals).

The evolution of peacebuilding comprises four main stages (see Richmond 2006: 217). Hyper-conservative, joint administration of colonial or quasi-colonial spaces by mainly European (but also American) imperial powers, with brute force being a viable but heavily disguised (i.e. counter-insurgency) method. The rise of the hegemonic ideal of non-violence challenged this hyper-conservative model though. Conservative notions of peacebuilding revolving around the ideal of a 'victor's peace' and 'constitutional peace' construed peacebuilding as a responsibility to intervene and establish a self-ruling 'post-conflict' order. 'Peace is a product of force and elite diplomacy' (ibid.) and accompanied by robust peacekeeping, mediation and truces. This was the hegemonic model of peacebuilding before and after World War II. The period since the 1960s has witnessed a constant widening of intervening actors and fields of intervention. Peacebuilding has shifted to some degree from force (or avoiding force as in peacekeeping) to more active measures revolving around notions of positive peace, thus supplementing constitutional peace with a widening agenda of 'institutional peace' that works through hegemony rather than force (as opposed to the victor's peace) and is concerned not only with self-determination and constitutionalization (as reflected in the UN Charter), but includes a much wider and longer-term engagement of the international community and local/national actors in various governance arenas: the economy, education, health etc. This 'peacebuilding consensus', that further profited from the end of the Cold War and the expectations that an 'Agenda for Peace' was now a realistic option for conflicts throughout the globe, underpins what is referred to in peace and conflict studies as the 'liberal peace', a 'peace constructed in conflict environment consensually through democratization, development, free-market reforms, human right, and the construction of civil society. External peacebuilders seek alliances with international actors as well as international sponsors' (ibid.: 193).

The liberal peace is not uncontested, however, not least because, as Autesserre (2009) points out, most peacebuilding endeavours fail to curtail violence, not least because the overall framing of peacebuilding neglects and Orientalizes local violence. That is why emerging semantics and practices of 'emancipatory peace' (MacGinty and Richmond 2013), based on an ontology of hybridity, local legitimacy and social justice, can be observed in many conflict sites, being advanced not only by more or less marginalized actors and taken up, although often in a superficial way, by hegemonic liberal peacebuilding actors. To sum up, hierarchical complexity with respect to peacebuilding as a main institutional complex of world politics figures in a change in – and generally speaking a widening of – its institutional contexts (global/UN, regional/regional organization, state-based multilateralism etc.), actor constellations (states, IOs, substate communities, international and national NGOs, local communities) and scales of intervention (broadly from negative peace to positive peace) in that context.

Coevolution and global peacebuilding

Finally, this internal differentiation of global peacebuilding, including the process of hierarchical complexity, does not happen in systemic isolation but rather in constant relation with development in other social realms. Four areas of coevolution arguably stand out.

Firstly, the coevolution between politics and science, exemplified by the fact that peace and conflict studies, like IR some decades earlier, has become, over time, a (highly interdisciplinary) discipline within the social sciences, attesting to a process of internal differentiation in the science system – the emergence of the discipline of IR taking place in a complex coevolution with the emergence of world politics (which is a good reason for backdating the core of IR theories to the nineteenth century, as Hobson (2012) does), and the emergence of peace and conflict studies post-World War II taking place in a complex coevolution with the institutional consolidation of liberal peacebuilding.

Secondly, the coevolution of world politics and international law, in particular in relation to the legal regulation of the problem of war and violence, a process that spans the period from the establishment of the International Red Cross following the battle of Solferino, to the Hague Conventions of 1899/1907, the Declaration of Human Rights and the UN Charter with its prohibition of the use of violence (except for carefully described exceptions) and the Rome Statute that led to the establishment of the International Criminal Court in 2002 – but also the development of soft law, such as the major human rights conventions of the 1960s and the notion of the 'responsibility to protect' that did, though, also serve as a justification for the NATO-led military intervention in Libya in 2011, a phenomenon that could also be read as contributing to the evolution of war, rather than that of peacebuilding.

Thirdly, the coevolution of world politics and the media system, which has a share in rendering the world a 'small place' in which violent conflicts elsewhere can be reported and decried, evoking political action to remedy them, and, not least, creates huge potential to rally concerned audiences from all over the globe that demand action for the sake of 'peace' (see Koloma Beck and Werron 2017: 284–285). And, fourthly, the coevolution of peacebuilding and learning/consciousness, expressed, for example, in global celebrations of peace as a human heritage. The Nobel peace prizes are an interesting case study here, not only because this is a form of social activism that is strongly institutionalized on a global scale, but also because the evolution of the awards shows precisely the shift to a growing range of activities (e.g. environmental protection, social justice and redistribution) and actors (earlier mainly statesmen, today also stateswomen and, in particular, non-state actors such as international organizations and individuals) that revolves, broadly speaking, around an evolution from proto-liberal, through liberal to emancipatory peace (Salmon 2002).

To conclude, one should keep in mind that, evolutionarily speaking, all these adaptations are precarious. Our analysis of how peacebuilding attests to an internal differentiation in world politics must not be read as an emancipatory story of how international politics contributes to overcoming violence. Quite the contrary. First of all, peacebuilding competes with other forms of internal differentiation, some of which are much more positively geared to the legitimized execution of violence for utilitarian objectives (war, nationalism, etc.). Secondly, peacebuilding always contains the possibility that violence will be legitimized either explicitly or implicitly. Thirdly, the mere existence of peacebuilding as a mode of observation that relies on identifying violent conflicts that have to be dealt with in the first place arguably supports the observation (and subjective impression) that over the long run world politics has not been getting more peaceful, but is shaped by theatres of violence that require urgent peacebuilding interventions.

4.3 The evolution of world politics through the practice of diplomacy

The example of peacebuilding in world politics reveals how historical trajectories that integrate 'old' ways of doing things into 'new' discursive frames – such as, for example, the balance of power and an ambivalent (legal) ideal of non-violence – contribute to the process of restabilization of world politics. However, 'old' forms do not simply disappear. The general evolutionary pattern – for as long as restabilization continues – is that they become more complex, leading to an increase not only in the overall complexity of social arrangements, but also in hierarchical forms of complexity that need to be processed discursively. Diplomacy and its contribution to the restabilization of world politics is a case in point. Diplomacy is the emergent stylized form of communication authorized by polity leaders that dates way back far into prehistory and that is attested in writings from the First Axial Age onwards. It is, therefore, a particularly promising site on which to trace hierarchical complexity. Since the mid-eighteenth century, the discursive marker 'new diplomacy' has characterized reflection on this phenomenon, and revolutionary as well as revisionist practices have defined the evolution of diplomacy ever since. Before we turn to a discussion of these developments, we wish to give some short examples of how the triad – variation, selection, restabilization – worked on cognitive models of diplomacy before the onset of modernity, focusing on how antecedent discursive layers were integrated into modern diplomatic practices.

We know a little about the evolution of diplomacy among hunter-gatherer bands from nineteenth- and twentieth-century studies of hunter-gatherers throughout the world (Neumann 2016; Numelin

1950). *Homo sapiens sapiens* lived in foraging bands of some 20 to 200 individuals since it emerged some 200,000 years ago, by which time *Homo sapiens* had already been doing the same since its emergence. These bands were dependent on a certain level of cooperation for finding and processing food, reproducing, etc. By archaeological consensus, the level of cooperation increased radically as a response to an environmental factor, namely the possibility of capturing big game. Regardless of the method of hunting adopted (driving animals into abysses, digging holes, spearing etc.), it would take a group rather than an individual to carry it out. The result of collaboration was pivotal in evolutionary terms, because it immediately led to a change in the unit of selection. With increased cooperation, the unit of selection changed from individual to group. For leading individuals, this revolution posed a challenge, for the superior individual hunting skills that had made them leaders were no longer an optimal environmental fit on their own, but had to be complemented by skills pertaining to leadership and collaboration. This change was driven by levelling behaviour, which meant that alpha males were lived down by coalitions that went in for sharing food, group sanctions and suchlike (compare Shostak 1976).

With the coming of agriculture (and, in select places, the possibility of establishing a stable food source from riparian resources), habitat density drove a selection process characterized by increased competition and also cooperation between polities. A pattern was initiated whereby culturally similar but politically distinct entities emerged. These polities interacted on a regular basis from territorially stable positions. The result was institutionalized patterns of interaction, which may be seen as the first embryonic diplomatic settings. We know of them from ethno-historical work, particularly on North America (Jennings 1985). As an example, consider the fifteenth- to nineteenth-century Iroquois Confederacy or League, or, more correctly, the Haudenosaunee (People of the Long-House). Their diplomacy was rooted in myth and centred on two loci, namely meetings at the wood's edge and, subsequently, in conference, around the campfire. Diplomacy focused on a particular form of messaging involving a kind of belt made of wampum (strings of beads or shells). Wampum holds considerable interest, for it is the best documented of what was possibly a number of techniques that could be drawn upon to conclude treaties before the advent of writing (another one is the knots or *quipo* of today's South America, a mnemonic system that may or may not share an origin with wampum). Considered as objects, wampum belts consisted of cylindrical beads made principally of shells drilled through from opposite ends. They were then strung in rows, forming a rectangular belt that was usually longer than it was wide. Colours conveyed meaning, with white symbolizing peace and life, black symbolizing war and death and so on. Belts were archived and could be read by specialists. Here we have early, rudimentary examples of treaties, archives and conferences.

Particularly in the seventeenth and eighteenth centuries, wampum played a key role in diplomacy, as it did in law-making. The importance of these belts went beyond graphic depiction, for the belt was said to carry the message of one council to another. These messages were literally read into the wampum before it was taken by a messenger to be presented to another tribal council (where the messenger lent the message voice). Diplomatic signalling took the form of making, presenting, receiving and handling the wampum. Words did not come alive without the help of the belts. Note that a spiritual, mythic realm must therefore be said to underwrite the wampum. From the seventeenth century onwards, as relations with English colonists took on increasing density, it also became increasingly wampum-based. Indeed, while the English definitely experienced this as a foreign practice, they took steps to make wampum more available and grasped that wampum was something that had to be learnt, and learnt well. This took time. On the basis of archival studies, Nancy Hagedorn (1988: 70) reports how, on more than one occasion, Iroquois delayed meetings with the English because the wampum sent beforehand was 'no more than Strings'. Hagedorn also details wampum's actual use in negotiations:

> the passing of a wampum string or belt punctuated each proposal or section of a speech. ... Once a belt had been received across the council fire, protocol demanded that similar belts or strings ac-

company each portion of the respondents' reply. When responding, the speaker displayed the received belts and strings in the order they were delivered by laying them upon a table or hanging them across a stick and repeating what was said on each. At the end of every article, he returned thanks, added his group's reply, and passed the new wampum across the fire. The return of the original belt without another one in reply indicated a rebuke or the rejection of the petitioners' proposal (ibid.: 66–67).

To the Iroquois, the wampum seems to have been to the spoken word what the written word is to the spoken word in literate cultures. In both cases, at formal occasions between two polities, the two go together. In both cases, the spoken word takes second place.

With the coming of writing and the First Axial Age, we can follow the evolution of these patterns in more detail (Podany 2010). A number of third-millennium archives on stone tablets with cuneiform inscriptions have come to light. Some of these tablets constitute surviving diplomatic exchanges between city-states. Up until the 1700s BCE, they circulated primarily in a Babylonian civilizational milieu. However, with the rise of the Hittite empire in the middle of that century, and with Egypt entering into denser contacts with its neighbouring states to the north, an intercivilizational diplomatic system came into being. IR scholars have now firmly established the so-called Amarna system as the world's first fully-fledged states system and the conventional bookend of historical scholarship. Its existence in the fourteenth century BCE is well documented, among other things through Pharaoh Akhenaten's (r. 1353–1336) library (Moran 1992). Diplomatic practices settled on ritualized exchanges between polity leaders who referred to one another by kinship terms (brothers, sons/fathers), enquired about one another's health and asked about gifts and favours. All this notably took place first in fourth-millennium BCE Sumerian and then in second-millennium BCE Akkadian, a language that by then was not the language of any of the polities involved (Babylonia, Egypt, Hatti, etc.; see Cohen and Westbrook 2000). This first large-scale diplomatic system disappeared with the late Bronze-age breakdown around 1200 BCE. A new formalized system emerged only some seven hundred years later, when the ancient Greeks formed institutions such as amphyctrionic leagues and Olympic Games. These institutions, whose primary purpose was to uphold cultic places (such as in Delphi) and make possible stylized and non-lethal competition, also served as diplomatic sites. Once again, however, this system was superseded and gave way to unilateral practices of approaching other polities, such as the Roman ones.

Although the Roman Empire was on many levels more differentiated than the Greek city-states, as far as diplomacy was concerned. hierarchical complexity was higher in Greece. This fact exemplifies our argument about the non-linearity and non-teleology of social evolution. Thus, Romans reverted to basic exchanges by messengers. The post-Roman world then came to know elaborate missions, where delivering a message was a function joined by the function of negotiation. These were called embassies. From the fourth century CE, different branches of Christendom saw the evolution of the institution of *apocrisiarii*, whereby some representatives of the Catholic Church were resident in Byzantine cities. The first permanent, reciprocal and fully-fledged example of secular leaders having resident representatives in other polities – what came to be known as permanent diplomacy – stems from the fifteenth-century Italian city-states system. This system selected permanent diplomats over messengers and embassies, to the extent that an embassy came to be the term not for a peripatetic, but a permanent mission. Diplomacy, as the umbrella within which diplomatic communications were processed, restabilized, in other words, as permanent diplomacy, a form that rapidly spread to cover all of Europe.

Before the Fourth Axial Age, the autonomization of diplomacy was negligible. A key reason for this was diplomacy's intimate co-evolution with religion. Like previous forms of diplomacy, European diplomacy was rooted in myth, more specifically in Christian founding myths. The world was seen as God's creation. God's will was seen to be that all humankind should live at peace with one another in a society anchored in religion. It followed that, when there was strife, it was because people were not living in accordance with God's will. Diplomacy, understood as the work of recreating the peaceful situation that God willed, was seen as a necessity in an imperfect world. People who specialized in reconstituting peace – and here we have one possible understanding of diplomats – were therefore doing God's work (Der Derian 1987). We have a wonderful example of how practices were rooted in myth and how this rooting may have been selected from the 1400s, the time when religiously defined Christendom began to transform into territorially defined Europe:

> Vladimir, Prince of Galitch, on being upbraided for not honouring a promise made on the cross of St Stephen, retorted that it had only been a very small cross, to which the complainant's envoy replied that it was nonetheless miraculous and that the Prince should be fearful for his life. (Hamilton and Langhorne 1995: 94)

Note that this interaction would have been impossible had there not existed a myth that laid down peaceful relations as the norm and a narrative sociability concerning the drawing up of promises, agreements and treaties, with specific ritual practices (the kissing of the cross was a practice which bound the kisser to the agreement entered into) and sanctions (heavenly punishment for breaking promises). Note, furthermore, that the myth and the practice are doxic and unchallengeable on their merits. Vladimir was reduced to quibbling over how ritual was performed rather than ritual as such, over adherence to a norm rather than the norm itself.

Autonomization

By the 1400s, with the diplomacy of Western Christendom well stabilized, variation raised its head again. Until 1455, diplomacy was conducted on a one-off basis, with an envoy and his entourage conducting a trip on behalf of one crowned head to another. That year, the Duke of Milan sent Nicodema de Pontremoli to Genoa in order to set up a permanent representation, for contacts had become so dense that a permanent presence made more sense than a series of intermittent visits. In about a century, most European states had such permanent representations. Whereas before, diplomats were courtiers and, as such, part of daily political life except when on embassies abroad, the fact that they were now away from court on a permanent basis singled them out as separate and gave them much more autonomy in their dealings with their host states. Previously, the same courtiers who were used for embassies abroad were often sent by the king to parley with his more exalted subjects; this practice was now wound down. Permanent embassies were, therefore, a key development in the autonomization of diplomacy. As non-European powers followed suit and established their own permanent embassies from the end of the eighteenth century onwards, the same autonomizing process was eventually in evidence throughout the globe.[8]

Autonomization was also strengthened by the emergence of what was to become known as the *corps diplomatique*. The emergence of permanent representation meant that ambassadors from different states regularly rubbed shoulders at the court to which they had been sent. Out of this grew the institution of the diplomatic corps, the totality of diplomats accredited to a particular sovereign at any one time considered as a body, for example, all the diplomats accredited to the Court of St. James's (that is, to the United Kingdom) or all the diplomats in Washington, DC. Traditionally, diplomats representing different sovereigns, particularly ambassadors, were rivals, and, although they tended to share an aristocratic background, there were few institutionalized cross-cutting bonds that made for solidarity. In 1556, England was already insisting that permanent ambassadors pay for their own lodgings. A century later, this was becoming a practice. The ensuing common material interest that foreign diplomats shared in seeing to it that their host country kept up its end of the bargain was clearly a factor making for solidarity, which further strengthened the *corps diplomatique* and, by extension, the autonomization of diplomacy as well.

Beginning in the mid-eighteenth century, the kind of highly stylized, permanent and secretive diplomacy that had by then been honed by aristocrats for 300 years came under direct attack. French Enlightenment philosophers presented a modern alternative, a

---

8   As so often, there were forerunners, such as the aforementioned *apocrisiarii*, representatives of the Catholic Church living with the Orthodox church, and Byzantine envoys sent to places like Kyiv at the end of the fourteenth century.

communicative variation, which they saw as a negation of old diplomacy. A 'no' is in evidence (Stetter 2014). This form of contestation is explained by Felix Gilbert, who points out that future foreign policy would entail a reversal of the diplomacy of the past, a new diplomacy:

> Relations among nations should follow moral laws. There should be no difference between the 'moral principles' which rule the relations among individuals and the 'moral principles' which rule relations between states. Diplomacy should be 'frank and open'. Formal treaties should be unnecessary; political alliances should be avoided particularly. Commercial conventions should refrain from all detailed regulations establishing individual advantages and privileges (Gilbert 1951: 15)

Here we have a clear example of normatively driven evolution. Note also the coevolution between the emergence of a postulated non-violent diplomacy focused on cooperation and peace and the emergence of a standard of peace as discussed in the previous section (3.2.). What was said in 3.2. about the importance of a certain constellation of the balance of power for the emergence of peace is equally relevant to the emergence of diplomacy. This diplomacy, which was characterized by its revolutionary French proponents as 'new', was briefly implemented (i.e. positively selected) by the revolutionary French regime, but was abolished (yet, as a negative selection, not forgotten) by the Directorate. It was, for example, the approach taken by early US diplomacy, only to resurface in 1919, when President Woodrow Wilson referred to the same alternative cognitive model of diplomacy as 'new', although by then it had been 'new' for some 150 years. A key aspect of this 'new' diplomacy came to be called multilateral diplomacy, diplomacy between more than one state.[9] Driven by increased social complexity but also by technological innovation in the area of communication, particularly

---

9   From an evolutionary perspective, it is particularly interesting to note that the meaning of the concept 'multilateral' seems to be changing, away from its basic descriptive meaning of diplomacy between more than two states, towards a richer meaning implying that no state may be barred from a mul-

in infrastructure, multilateral diplomacy became increasingly formalized in international organizations. As evolutionary phenomena always do, these international organizations had precursors, arguably stretching back all the way to hunter-gatherer meetings, as it were. More complex forms of multilateral diplomacy emerged with the irregular church meetings of the Catholic Church from the fourth century onwards and the kurultais that were called to choose successor rulers in the Turko-Mongol tradition of Eurasian steppe politics. Even more elaborate comings together of states such as the Congress of Augsburg (1555), the Congress of Westphalia (1648), the Congress of Vienna (1815) were then called to settle new orders after wars.

Hierarchical complexity

In the years after the Congress of Vienna, there was an attempt made to establish Congresses on a permanent basis, the so-called Concert of Europe. It was in operation formally from 1815 to 1822, when it met annually, and went on informally for decades thereafter. The point here was that the Great Powers met to settle matters that they perceived as threatening the European order, as in the expression 'working in concert'. The formal division of states into small and great powers that had taken place at the Congress of Vienna and that made the Congress of Europe possible, consecrated the hierarchization that had been in evidence since the autonomization of diplomacy. During the eighteenth century, for example, it fell to great powers to guarantee treaties between minor ones. At Vienna, great powers arrogated to themselves the right to exchange diplomats with the rank of ambassadors; all diplomats exchanged by smaller powers had to use other titles, such as minister.[10]

---

tilateral set-up. Inclusiveness makes for denser relations, so this is a trend to follow.

10   With reference to what was said about the functional-structuralist character of Waltz's (1979) theory of structural realism above, note that, as far as diplomacy is concerned, there is a direct parallel between what Waltz talks about as the third layer of his generative model of the system and calls the

With the founding of the League of Nations in 1919, permanent multilateral diplomacy went global. The League of Nations itself was not a functional organization, but a general one. It combined features both of early Congresses (broad membership, overarching working area) and extant international organizations. Furthermore, the League served as a spawning site for new functional organizations, such as the International Studies Conference, where people who studied International Relations met, coordinated ongoing activities and initiated new ones. International organizations covering more and more specific activities came into being. Whereas former historians of the League tended to foreground its failure, most historians now think more in evolutionary terms and focus on the League's role as harbinger of the United Nations. Both organizations demonstrate the further evolution and densification of world society. The work of the perhaps hundred thousand international organizations that exist today has increased the number of people doing diplomatic work enormously and has lent global diplomacy a much, much more socially dense quality than it had only a hundred years ago. Whereas four-digit numbers sufficed to count the diplomats on the eve of the First World War, diplomats working for states today are reckoned in six-digit numbers, and if we add international civil servants, activists in non-governmental organizations, consultants, spin doctors and so on, we probably reach a seven-digit number. We will come back to the role of coevolution with the growth in state bureaucracies as a precondition for this development. As far as hierarchization is concerned, note that the United Nations has actually institutionalized the tension between diplomacy amongst sovereign and hence formally equal states on the one hand, and diplomacy as unequal exchange on the other. The UN's General Assembly works on the premise on the former; the UN Security Council on the premise of the latter. Note also that the growing autonomization of diplomacy goes hand in hand with its continued hierarchization. Perhaps lingering hierarchization is

---

'differentiation of power capabilities' on the one hand, and what we call hierarchization on the other.

even a precondition for autonomization, for in this way, great powers retain an indirect possibility of governing diplomatic processes that they would not have had without it. The possibility of indirect control makes it possible to renounce some of the possibilities of direct control, which evaporate with the increased autonomization of diplomacy (compare Neumann and Sending 2010).

On the global level, the relationship between what we might call 'old' and 'new' diplomacy over the last 250 years or so is a good example of the variation and hierarchical complexity that is shaped by the ambivalence between these different forms of diplomacy and attests to the way in which the tension between the two shapes the constant restabilization of world politics as an autonomous social realm.[11] There is a general point to be made here. So far, old and new diplomacies have simply not diverged enough to be treated as two variants of diplomacy in an evolutionary sense. For that to happen, there would have to be changes in the principle that grounds both these styles of diplomacy. That principle is sovereignty, which, during the nineteenth and twentieth centuries, broadened to become a global principle of political organization. Sovereignty remains the key phenomenon framing the social and material environment within which diplomacy develops. Sovereignty itself, however, is not a phenomenon that stands still to have its picture taken. On the one hand, we see a traditional variant of sovereignty that insists on a world of clear boundaries between states that can always use their sovereign power to keep what is inside them separate from outside elements. Sovereignty is rooted in the state, which rules by bidding other entities to carry out its will. On the other hand, we see a newer version of sovereignty that insists on a world of

---

11   This also includes the emergence and global spread of permanent multilateral diplomacy, in particular the emergence of IOs since the nineteenth century. In that context, the number of diplomats and quasi-diplomats working for states, IOs, NGOs, etc. rose from four-digit numbers prior to World War I to probably seven-digit numbers today, thereby adding more and more layers of hierarchical complexity to diplomacy in the system of world politics, not least by involving an ever-growing number of actors in global peacebuilding.

permeable boundaries between states that try to handle the ensuing flows between what lies inside and what lies outside them. This kind of sovereignty is rooted in the international community, the state citizens of which partake in global governance through other kinds of polities such as non-governmental organizations, companies etc. If we map the old and new diplomacy onto these two variants of sovereignty, the fit is quite striking. State sovereignty grounds old diplomacy. Historically, the two have a complicated relationship, for in the eighteenth century the King's diplomacy was a major target for those who argued that sovereignty should be popular. Today, however, the principle of popular sovereignty is well ensconced, and is grounding diplomacy quite frictionlessly. The preponderance of old diplomacy is also helped by the changing balance of power. Most political forces in China and India are, in their different ways, following the broad understanding of sovereignty that grounds old diplomacy. Old diplomacy with its *faits accomplis* is, for example, on ample display in the South China Sea, where China keeps on creating new land at a brisk pace. Furthermore, and as already noted, in the face of stiffer competition from China, India and also Russia, the United States seems increasingly to follow the practices of old diplomacy as well.

And yet, stabilization around old diplomacy is not in sight, and is unlikely to take place, simply because too many well-ensconced 'new' diplomatic practices exist that are at variance with it. Within Europe, diplomacy has undergone a radical transformation in the form of the EU and its Brussels-based and committee-centred decision-making mechanism, while the 'old' form of bilateral diplomacy between EU member states endures in parallel. In the interstices between Europe and its neighbours, variation and hegemonic complexity can be witnessed on a running basis. Russia's 2014 invasion and incorporation of Ukraine's Crimean peninsula may serve as an example. The takeover and its diplomatic follow-up were a clearcut example of what, in terms of the old diplomacy, is known as a *fait accompli* (Constantinou 1996). The idea is to have one's way by presenting other states with an arm-twisting shock rather than aiming for the diplomatic practice of a prenegotiated solution. The action was seen by many Western leaders not only as illegal, but as tellingly outdated. German Chancellor Angela Merkel reportedly told US President Barack Obama in a telephone conversation that 'Putin lives in another world' – a world that many Western leaders thought had been left behind (Fleischhauer 2014). What Merkel described here may be read in evolutionary terms as fatigue with the burden of a hierarchical complexity that one cannot get rid of, as dramatically underlined by the war between Russia and Ukraine that began in 2022. The drama of social evolution in which these actors are performing may be captured in the social evolutionary terms that we have drawn upon here. However, it is simply rooted in too deep a social shift away from the one-off interest-based games that characterized eighteenth-century interaction between states (still favoured by Putin) towards the iterative multilateral games (preferred by Merkel and Obama) to be captured by Tang's (2013) much more linear argument about a shift away from offensive towards defensive realism. Adler's (2019) focus on collaborative world-making would also struggle to capture what we have highlighted here, for the simple reason that his approach downplays the intensity and drawn-out temporality of the social struggles (and entrenched hierarchies) that often surround evolutionary selection.

Coevolution

The denser the information exchange within a system, the greater the perceived need for its units to formalize that information. There is a clear coevolution between the growth of systems density on the one hand, and the autonomization of diplomacy on the other, so much so that the autonomization of diplomacy and the widening and broadening of its field of operation have to be seen as constitutive of the system. A functionalist example would be how, first after the Napoleonic Wars and the Congress of Vienna and then after the Crimean War, what came to be known as fully-fledged 'international' organizations (i.e. organizations with states as members) emerged, such as the Central Commission for Navigation on the Rhine (1815) and its equivalent on the Danube (1856; Yao 2022). They still exist, with the former having a membership of five states, a permanent secretariat in Strasbourg and a staff with a dozen plus members.

Towards the end of the nineteenth century, these international organizations were joined by functional ones, such as the International Telegraph Union (originally the International Telegraph Convention, 1865, now a UN agency) and the International Postal Union (1874), which brought permanence to multinational diplomacy, just as permanence had been brought to bilateral diplomacy some centuries before. The emergence of these international organizations, which were also a precondition for the emergence of first the League of Nations and then the United Nations and indeed for permanent multilateral diplomacy of all kinds, must be seen in the context of coevolution between diplomacy on the one hand, understood as speaking to the other, and bureaucracy on the other, understood as a way of administering functional processes. Another example of the same type of coevolution can be found in the emergence of foreign ministries in Europe from the end of the eighteenth century onwards, and then across the globe. In this case, coevolution did not involve international, but national bureaucratic processes.

Coevolution with knowledge production is in evidence first and foremost with respect to international law. The standardization of who could send and receive diplomats and which titles they were supposed to use as well as the legal recognition of the *corps diplomatique* that took place at the Congress of Vienna was a clear turning point. A body of diplomatic law began to grow, with the Vienna Convention on Diplomatic Relations of 1961 and its twin on consular relations of 1963 being particularly noteworthy developments. The pursuit of social scientific study of diplomacy only took off some three decades ago, which is probably too short a time span for this to be a notable development in evolutionary terms.

Coevolution with the media has become increasingly important. Diplomatic press offices emerged in the interwar period, as part and parcel of so-called public diplomacy. Public diplomacy concerns attempts by the diplomats of one state to influence another state's agency by appealing directly and/or indirectly to that state's citizens. It was pioneered by revolutionary states, especially the United States and, a long century later, the Soviet Union, and is now mimicked by most other states. Note also how national and international media have come to hold an agenda-setting function over diplomacy, particularly in states with a fairly free press, to the extent that agendas at morning meetings in a number of foreign ministries often mirror press activity directly.

5 Social evolution and knowing world politics

In the interest of furthering our understanding of world politics, this book has presented an ambitious assemblage of theories. However, it has not presented a theory of world or international politics – at least not in the conventional senses in which 'IR theory' is understood in the discipline of International Relations. It has rather argued that social evolutionary theory provides an extremely powerful tool for understanding world politics in a wider societal and long-term historical context. In fact, we have argued that social evolutionary theorizing only makes sense if set in the context of comprehensive theories of society that contain within them a basic trajectory of social evolutionary analysis. In our case, that primarily meant the theories of Foucault, Habermas and Luhmann. It also means that social evolutionary analysis can be applied to any part of the social world (say rock music, religious belief systems, scientific theories, forms of organizing the economy, social etiquette and so on), and not merely to world politics. However, given the state in which we found theorizing in IR, we have to conclude that much work remains to be done. There is a glaring lack of studies of deep historical change within the discipline, particularly when it comes to studies of deep historical change that are actually informed by comprehensive social theories (and thus draw on the body of systematic work associated with the theory in question, rather than on the work of any particular fashionable thinker). Notable philosophical and anthropological knowledge bases that are readily available have, as of now, simply not been put to use.

We have addressed this lack of deep history and social theory in most approaches to evolutionary thinking in IR in the preceding chapters and have, more importantly, presented our own take on it, combining (continental European) social theory with an empirical reflection on the evolution of axial ages. By way of summarizing our main line of argument we now turn the spotlight on the three principal areas in which our thinking has unfolded.

Firstly, as far as deep history is concerned, we have delved into Karl Jaspers' philosophical and Jan Assmann's empirical-archaeological notion of the Axial Age and transformed it into a reading of the coevolution of social evolutionary theories and social structure. Within that conjoined context we have identified four stages that could be read from an evolutionary standpoint in terms of their hierarchical complexity. The first of these comprises a pre-Axial age (of classical segmentary, presedentary societies) and first Axial Age (of the first city-states and script-based cultures) that, very much in contrast to the common view of them as unrelated to modern civilization, appeared as large-scale social laboratories in which a basic idea of humanity and social contracts between humans prospered. Taking our cue from the work of Christopher Boehm, we identified the notion of cultural learning and the institutionalization of 'reverse dominance hierarchy' as the defining and enduring feature of myths (i.e. proto-theories of evolution) and social structures built on egalitarianism and freedom – evolutionary groundwork for millennia to come.

The Second Axial Age ('*the* Axial Age' for Jaspers and Assmann) then set in with the selection and restabilization of hierarchical societies, stratified within and taking the form of (imperial) centres and peripheries in inter-polity relations. On the level of myths and proto-social theory, the memory of egalitarianism and fundamental freedom allowed people to conceive of counter-present change, as evident in core texts such as the *Odyssey* and Exodus and also prevalent in the Eastern tradition from Zoroastrian thought to Buddhism. Over time, and notably in early Christianity, counter-present theorizing challenged hierarchical societies by providing an alternative master image, one based on a memory of universalism reaching back far into the (pre-script) past. These counter-present and largely transcendent notions of equality, visible inter alia in Axial Age spiritual and textual traditions as well as in early Christianity, then turned immanent in what we have termed the Third Axial Age. In the Papal Revolutions of the eleventh century – as well as in parallel processes such as in early Islamic polities – change was theorized as an inner-worldly possibility that needed to be rationally and legally organized. This, then, was the age of proto-functional differentiation in the Western Christian realm, but also in the Califates. In contemporary terminology it witnessed the codification of norms and ideas that revolved around a principle of human-made law and based the social contract on legal relations of (at least theoretical) equality between subjects or souls. This kick-off period of functional differentiation then evolved into the Fourth Axial Age of global constitutionalism, which is planetary in scale. In line with world society theories we can, at this stage, only speculate as to the extent to which the, at first sporadic and then permanent, interpenetration and entanglement of people and cultures across the entire globe, with all the forms of inequality, violence and hierarchy that involved, shaped this process. There is a heightened possibility of observing differences in equality. One example concerns ideas about 'equality' and 'freedom' in what we referred to as the Fourth Axial Age of global constitutionalism in section 2. These range from the Nakaz written in Russia by Catherine the Great in 1767 to the French Revolution. The whole range stands in contrast to a widespread perception that freedom and universalism travels from West to East, for by the time of the French revolution the Nakaz was well known in France too. More broadly, there existed global patterns of observation and inspiration that shaped the Atlantic revolutions from the USA to France and Haiti (and back). These might have been evolutionary preconditions for unleashing the evolutionary selection of functional differentiation visible in the increasing autonomization of various social spheres of what is today termed global modernity. Self-legislation in terms of positive law, constitutionalism and an increasingly complex and self-referential legal sphere and the self-representation visible in democratic, semi-democratic and authoritarian forms of political rule based on ideas of self-determination, progress and citizenship are the defining feature of this evolutionary stage.

Secondly, social structure and social theory coevolve and, as a result, it probably comes as no surprise that as part of an autonomization of science in the context of functional differentiation explicitly evolutionary theories emerged, first in the natural sciences but then also, as we have shown, in the social sciences. Central to our argument is, however, that the two should be clearly separated. Theories of natural evolution do not explain social evolution. Social evolution involves, but is not driven by, cognitive evolution. To substantiate this argument, we have identified and elaborated on a complementarity in social evolutionary thinking in the social theories of Michel Foucault, Jürgen Habermas and Niklas Luhmann – also hoping to end the persistent misperception, not least in IR, that these social theories fundamentally differ. Of course, there are differences between these writers, just as there are differences in the evolution of each of these writers' individual thoughts over time. The shared paradigm between them that we have identified, however, rests on two pillars central to modern social evolutionary thinking and unique to social, as opposed to both natural and cognitive, evolution. On the one hand, communication (discourse, etc.) is identified, from a constructivist point of view, as what evolves in social evolution in the first place; on the other hand, its complexity is expressed in the triad of variation, selection and restabilization, the fundamental sequence of all forms of evolution including social evolution. Moreover, we then identified three structural effects of social evolution which we defined as autonomization (in particular of social spheres), hierarchical complexity (between and within social spheres) and coevolution (between social spheres).

Thirdly, we regard this identification of how evolution shapes social structures and social theories not as a dry, detached theoretical affair but as a highly relevant means of moving IR theorizing onto new territory. We have no wish to repeat what we have already argued in relation to the emergence of the modern system of world politics, peacebuilding and diplomacy. The key point is simply that the story told above could be told by looking at different elements of the system of world politics, as we did in section 4 or, instead, by identifying core features of evolutionary theory and how they play out in world politics. Doing the latter

- shows how autonomization figures in the internal differentiation of world politics, with the selection and restabilization of a distinct international (sub)system of world politics based on the communicative marker of balance of power. But it also includes the internal differentiation of this system in which, for example, an ideal of non-violence functions as a trigger for the internal autonomization of peacebuilding as a distinct sphere of action and the (functional) necessity of establishing permanent communicative structures leads to the selection of modern diplomacy as an antecedent to a fully-fledged system of world politics.
- shapes hierarchical complexity in relation to the three cases discussed in section 4, to wit, the struggle over hegemonic forms of organizing political authority in which nation-states – some of them possessing great power/imperial capacities – took precedence. Other variations, however, set in too, in particular with the establishment of international organizations as arenas of authority. This becomes visible when we look at the hierarchical complexity involved in the evolution of the notions of liberal peace prevalent since the nineteenth century and the fluctuation between old and new diplomacy.
- and finally reveals how coevolution, in particular with (international) law, was central to all three empirical illustrations, from 'classical' international law, to humanitarian law, human rights law and diplomatic protocol as well as, let us not forget, the coevolution between these changes in the political world, on the one hand, and their academic and scientific observation, on the other. Without an autonomization of a system of world politics there would be no IR and no IR theory. Peace and Conflict Studies developed in relation to ongoing political endeavours to engage with political structures linked to an ideal of non-violence. And, although this is a little speculative, the social scientific study of diplomacy is driven by an increasing complexity regarding who exactly is involved in diplomacy, from states, international organizations, NGOs to individuals. However, this is not to suggest a relationship that goes in one direction only, in the sense that the evolution of world politics shapes the evolution of the (social)

sciences. Rather, both conservative and critical approaches to the very setup of world politics – say from the realist angle on the one hand to the post-colonial on the other (and at times even from that of an odd geopolitical mélange of the two) – wander from classrooms into official jargon, foreign ministries, think tanks, military academies and 'popular' beliefs about what world politics is all about. Notions of negative and positive peace have become standardized and translated into political concepts, while functional theories of interdependence arguably render the establishment of international organizations plausible as well as a greater say for substate actors in world politics – and once they are around, it is a short step to theorizing their actorhood as an invitation to enrich prevailing notions of diplomacy.

What follows from this seems to be quite simple. In order to understand world politics, three things need to be done together: to look into deep history; to muster the theory required to do so; and to refrain from reinventing the wheel by drawing instead on extant studies from other disciplines. We have also proposed a way in which this can be done by applying social evolutionary theory. Of course, we ultimately leave it to readers to judge how inspiring they find this approach in general, and as a tool for their own research in particular. However, what should also be noted is that deeply embedded in the current project lies a programmatic statement on a scientific undertaking as well as on disciplinary politics. We argue that understanding world politics ultimately will not thrive by the academic discipline of International Relations integrating theories, approaches and thinkers into its own orbit and the fields of its self-referential theoretical 'campfires'. Such pastimes are very selective and tend to lead nowhere. What is needed is, rather, a broader understanding of how world politics requires bringing the knowledge base of International Relations *together* with those of other fields and disciplines. A transdisciplinarity of this kind would be intellectually and analytically rewarding, even though it would be an extremely demanding and difficult exercise. Compared to such a Herculean task, what we have presented in this book is simply a charting of the waters. Still, we are convinced that pursuing such a transdisciplinary approach, however imperfectly, has only been possible because, as individual authors working in IR, sociology, anthropology, (international) law, area studies and philosophy (and the various interstices between these disciplines and others, most notably history), we have been wandering off the most well-trodden paths of intradisciplinary debates peculiar to IR for quite some time already, only to then bring together the results of these individual and quite diverse wanderings in what has been a long and stimulating cowriting and discussion process. We should emphasize that this process has been going on for a decade and that, although never planned in this way, it has turned out to be very much a 'framework process' where the discussions condensed in the present book both informed and benefitted from work that its individual authors had been doing over these years, and how our own thinking on evolution evolved in that process. It is in this sense that we understand this book to be not only a proposal for the use of social evolutionary theory for understanding world politics, but also as an argument for the benefits of in-depth, if demanding, cross-disciplinary engagement. We regard it as an appreciation of this kind of coevolving cooperation.

References

Adler, Emanuel 1991. Cognitive Evolution: A Dynamic Approach for the Study of International Relations and Their Progress. In: *Progress in Postwar International Relations*, edited by Emanuel Adler and Beverly Crawford, 43–88. New York: Columbia University Press.

Adler, Emanuel 2019. *World Ordering: A Social Theory of Cognitive Evolution*. Cambridge: Cambridge University Press.

Adorno, Theodor W. 1975. *Negative Dialektik*. Frankfurt a.M.: Suhrkamp.

Åkerstrøm Andersen, Niels 2003. *Discursive Analytical Strategies: Understanding Foucault, Koselleck, Laclau, Luhmann*. Bristol: Policy Press.

Akira, Iriye, Petra Goedde and William I. Hitchcock (eds.) 2012. *The Human Rights Revolution: An International History*. Oxford: Oxford University Press.

Albert, Mathias 2002. *Zur Politik der Weltgesellschaft: Identität und Recht im Kontext globaler Vergesellschaftung*. Weilerswist: Velbrück.

Albert, Mathias 2016. *A Theory of World Politics*. Cambridge: Cambridge University Press.

Albert, Mathias and Barry Buzan 2010. Differentiation: A Sociological Approach to International Relations Theory. *European Journal of International Relations* 16 (3): 315–337.

Albert, Mathias, Oliver Kessler and Stephan Stetter 2008. On Order and Conflict: International Relations and the 'Communicative Turn'. *Review of International Studies* 34 (1): 43–67.

Almeida, Fabio 2014. The Emergence of Constitutionalism as an Evolutionary Adaptation. *Cardozo Public Law, Policy, and Ethics Journal* 13 (1): 1–96.

Amstutz, Marc and Andreas Fischer-Lescano (eds.) 2013. *Kritische Systemtheorie: Zur Evolution einer normativen Theorie*. Bielefeld: transcript.

Apel, Karl-Otto 2011. *Paradigmen der Ersten Philosophie: Zur reflexiven – transzendentalpragmatischen – Rekonstruktion der Philosophiegeschichte*. Berlin: Suhrkamp.

Arnold, John H. 2009. Religion and Popular Rebellion, from the Capuciati to Niklashausen. *Cultural and Social History* 6 (2): 1–20.

Assmann, Jan 1990. *Ma'at – Gerechtigkeit und Unsterblichkeit im Alten Ägypten*. München: Beck.

Assmann, Jan 1995. *Politische Theologie zwischen Ägypten und Israel*. München: Siemens-Stiftung.

Assmann, Jan 2013. *Das kulturelle Gedächtnis: Schrift, Erinnerung und politische Identität in frühen Hochkulturen*. München: Beck.

Assmann, Jan 2015. *Exodus. Die Revolution der Alten Welt*. München: Beck.

Assmann, Jan 2018. *Achsenzeit: Eine Archäologie der Moderne*. München: Beck.

Autesserre, Séverine 2009. Hobbes and the Congo: Frames, Local Violence, and International Intervention. *International Organization* 63 (2): 249–280.

Baecker, Dirk (ed.) 2021. *Schlüsselwerke der Systemtheorie*. Wiesbaden: Springer VS.

Bartelson, Jens 2017. *War in International Thought*. Cambridge: Cambridge University Press.

Bauer, Thomas 2018. *Warum es kein islamisches Mittelalter gab: Das Erbe der Antike und des Orient*. München: Beck.

Beckman, Gary 1999. *Hittite Diplomatic Texts*. Atlanta, GA: Scholars Press.

Berman, Harold J. 1985. *Law and Revolution: The Formation of the Western Legal Tradition*. Cambridge, MA: Harvard University Press.

Berman, Harold J. 1991. *Recht und Revolution: Die Bildung der westlichen Rechtstradition*. Frankfurt a.M.: Suhrkamp.

Blickle, Peter 2003. *Von der Leibeigenschaft zu den Menschenrechten: Eine Geschichte der Freiheit in Deutschland*. München: Beck.

Blickle, Peter 2004. *Die Revolution von 1525*. München: Oldenbourg.

Boehm, Christopher 1993. Egalitarian Behavior and Reverse Dominance Hierarchy. *Current Anthropology* 34 (3): 227–254.

Boehm, Christopher 2001. *Hierarchy in the Forest. The Evolution of Egalitarian Behavior*. Cambridge, MA: Harvard University Press.

Boesch, Christophe 2012. *Wild Cultures: A Comparison between Chimpanzee and Human Cultures*. Cambridge: Cambridge University Press.

Bohannan, Laura 1978. Politische Führerschaft bei den Tiv. In: *Das Stammessystem der Nuer im südlichen Sudan*, edited by Fritz Kramer and Christian Sigrist, 226–230. Frankfurt: Syndikat.

Borch, Christian 2005. Systemic Power: Luhmann, Foucault and Analytics of Power. *Acta Sociologica* 48 (2): 155–167.

Bouchard, Frédéric and Philippe Huneman (eds.) 2013. *From Groups to Individuals: Evolution and Emerging Individuality*. Cambridge, MA: MIT Press.

Bourke, Andrew F.G. 2011. *Principles of Social Evolution*. Oxford: Oxford University Press.

Brandom, Robert 1994. *Reasoning, Representing, and Discursive Commitment*. Cambridge, MA: Harvard University Press.

Breuer, Stefan 1994. Kulturen der Achsenzeit: Leistung und Grenzen eines geschichtsphilosophischen Konzepts. *Saeculum* 45 (1): 1–33.

Bright, Charles and Michael Geyer 2001. Benchmarks of Globalization: The Global Condition, 1850–2010. In: *A Companion to World History*, edited by Douglas Northrop, 285–300. Chichester: John Wiley.

Brown, Peter 1989. Spätantike. In: *Geschichte des privaten Lebens 1: Vom Römischen Imperium bis zum Byzantinischen Reich*, edited by Paul Veyne, 229–297. Frankfurt a.M.: Fischer.

Brown, Peter 2002. *Poverty and Leadership in the Later Roman Empire*. Waltham, MA: Brandeis University Press.

Brundage James A. and Melodie H. Eichbauer 2022. *Medieval Canon Law*. London: Routledge.

Brunkhorst, Hauke 2005. *Solidarity: From Civic Friendship to a Global Legal Community*. Cambridge, MA: MIT Press.

Brunkhorst, Hauke 2014. *Critical Theory of Legal Revolutions: Evolutionary Perspectives*. New York: Bloomsbury Publishing.

Buber, Martin 2014. Königtum Gottes. In: *Werkausgabe: Schriften zum Messianismus*, edited by Samuel H. Brody, 93–276. Gütersloh: Gütersloher Verlagshaus.

Bucher, Bernd and Julian Eckl 2021. Football's Contribution to International Order: The Ludic and Festive Reproduction of International Society by World Society Actors. *International Theory* 14 (2): 311–337.

Bull, Hedley 1977. *The Anarchical Society: A Study of Order in World Politics*. London: Macmillan.

Butler, William E. and Wladimir A. Tomsinov 2009. *The Nakaz of Catherine the Great: Collected Texts*. Clark: The Lawbook Exchange.

Buzan, Barry 2004. *From International to World Society? English School Theory and the Social Structure of Globalisation*. Cambridge: Cambridge University Press.

Buzan, Barry 2014. The 'Standard of Civilisation' as an English School Concept. *Millennium: Journal of International Studies* 42 (3): 576–594.

Buzan, Barry 2023. *Making Global Society: A Study of Humankind Across Three Eras*. Cambridge: Cambridge University Press.

Buzan, Barry, Charles Jones and Richard Little 1993. *The Logic of Anarchy: Neorealism to Structural Realism*. New York: Columbia University Press.

Buzan, Barry and George Lawson 2014. Rethinking Benchmark Dates in International Relations. *European Journal of International Relations* 20 (2): 437–462.

Buzan, Barry and Richard Little 2000. *International Systems in World History: Remaking the Study of International Relations*. Oxford: Oxford University Press.

Buzan, Barry and Ole Wæver 2005. *Regions and Powers: The Structure of International Security*. Cambridge: Cambridge University Press.

Buzan, Barry and George Lawson 2015. *The Global Transformation: History, Modernity and the Making of International Relations*. Cambridge: Cambridge University Press.

Caner, Daniel 2021. *The Rich and the Pure: Philanthropy and the Making of Christian Society in Early Byzantium*. Oakland, CA: University of California Press.

Carey, Nessa 2012. *The Epigenetic Revolution: How Modern Biology is Rewriting Our Understanding of Genetics, Disease, and Inheritance*. New York: Columbia University Press.

Cashdan, Elizabeth A. 1980. Egalitarianism among Hunters and Gatherers. *American Anthropologist* 82 (1): 116–120.

Cassirer, Ernst 1994. *Das Erkenntnisproblem in der Philosophie der Neueren Zeit*. Darmstadt: Wissenschaftliche Buchgesellschaft.

Cassirer, Ernst 2013. *Individuum und Kosmos in der Philosophie der Renaissance*. Hamburg: Meiner.

Clastres, Pierre 1974. *La société contre l'état*. Paris: Édition de Minuit.

Cohen, Raymond and Raymond Westbrook (eds.) 2000. *Amarna Diplomacy: The Beginnings of International Relations*. Baltimore, MD: Johns Hopkins University Press.

Colley, Linda 2021. *The Gun, the Ship and the Pen: Warfare, Constitutions and the Making of the Modern World*. London: Profile.

Commons, Michael and Sara Ross 2008. The Hierarchical Complexity View of Evolution and History. *World Futures* 64 (5/7): 399–405.

Constantinou, Costas 1996. *On The Way to Diplomacy*. Minneapolis, MN: University of Minnesota Press.

Dawkins, Richard 1976. *The Selfish Gene*. Oxford: Oxford University Press.

De Carvalho, Benjamin, Halvard Leira and John M. Hobson 2011. The Big Bangs of IR: The Myths That Your Teachers Still Tell You about 1648 and 1919. *Millennium: Journal of International Studies* 39 (3): 35–58.

De Waal, Frans 1982. *Chimpanzee Politics: Power and Sex among Apes*. New York: Harper and Row.

Dennett, Daniel C. 2017. *From Bacteria to Bach and Back: The Evolution of Minds*. New York: Penguin.

Der Derian, James 1987. *On Diplomacy. A Genealogy of Western Estrangement*. Oxford: Blackwell.

Deudney, Daniel 2020. *Dark Skies*. Princeton, NJ: Princeton University Press.

Deutsch, Karl W. 1966. *The Analysis of International Relations*. Eaglewood Cliffs, NJ: Prentice-Hall.

Dewey, John 1925. *Experience and Nature*. Chicago, IL: Open Court Publishing.

Diamond, Jared 2005. *Collapse: How Societies Choose to Fail or Succeed*. New York: Penguin.

Dick, Steven J. and Mark L. Lupisella eds. 2009. *Cosmos and Culture: Cultural Evolution in a Cosmic Context*. Washington, DC: NASA.

Duby, Georges 1981. *Die drei Ordnungen*. Frankfurt a.M.: Suhrkamp.

Duby, Georges 2020. *Zeit der Kathedralen: Kunst und Gesellschaft 980–1420*. Frankfurt a.M.: Suhrkamp.

Durkheim, Émile 1933. *The Division of Labor in Society*. Glencoe, IL: Free Press.

Eberl, Oliver 2021. *Naturzustand und Barbarei: Begründung und Kritik staatlicher Ordnung im Zeichen des Kolonialismus*. Hamburg: Hamburger Edition.

Eberl, Oliver and Peter Niesen 2022. *Immanuel Kant: Zum ewigen Frieden. Kommentar von Oliver Eberl und Peter Niesen*. Frankfurt a.M.: Suhrkamp.

Eisenstadt, Shmuel N. 1987. *Kulturen der Achsenzeit II*. Frankfurt a.M.: Suhrkamp.

Elias, Norbert 1976. *Über den Prozeß der Zivilisation: Soziogenetische und psychogenetische Untersuchungen*. Frankfurt a.M.: Suhrkamp.

Emerson, Ralph W. 1983. *Essays and Lectures*. New York: Library of America.

Emirbayer, Mustafa 1997: Manifesto for a Relational Sociology. *American Journal of Sociology* 103 (2): 281–317.

Fassbender, Bardo 2009. *The United Nations Charter as the Constitution of the International Community*. Leiden and Boston: Nijhoff.

Fetscher, Iring 1960. Der gesellschaftliche 'Naturzustand' und das Menschenbild bei Hobbes, Pufendorf, Cumberland und Rousseau: Ein Beitrag zur Standortbestimmung der politischen Theorie Rousseaus. *Schmollers Jahrbuch für Gesetzgebung, Verwaltung und Volkswirtschaft* 80 (2): 641–685.

Flasch, Kurt 1994. *Einführung in die Philosophie des Mittelalters*. Darmstadt: Wissenschaftliche Buchgesellschaft.

Flasch, Kurt 2006. *Das philosophische Denken im Mittelalter: Von Augustin bis Machiavelli*. Stuttgart: Reclam.

Fleischhauer, Jan 2014. Russlands Realitätsverlust. *Spiegel Online*, available at: https://www.spiegel.de/politik/ausland/mh17-malaysia-airlines-putins-wirklichkeitsverlust-a-9823-25.html [accessed 10th February 2021].

Foucault, Michel 1972. *The Archaeology of Knowledge*. New York: Pantheon Books.

Foucault, Michel 1994. *Dits et Écrits IV: 1954–1988*. Paris: Gallimard.

Foucault, Michel 2003. *Society Must be Defended: Lectures at the Collège de France, 1975–76*. London: Penguin.

Foucault, Michel 2008. *Security, Territory, Population: Lectures at The Collège de France, 1977–78*. Basingstoke: Palgrave.

Foucault, Michel 2020. *Discipline and Punish: The Birth of the Prison*. London: Penguin.

Fried, Johannes 1974. *Die Entstehung des Juristenstandes im 12. Jahrhundert*. Köln: Böhlau.

Fried, Johannes 2007. Über den Universalismus der Freiheit im Mittelalter. In: *Zu Gast im Mittelalter*, edited by Johannes Fried, 143–173. München: Beck.

Galtung, Johan 1969. Violence, Peace, and Peace Research. *Journal of Peace Research* 6 (3): 167–191.

Gardner, Peter M. 1991. Forager's Pursuit of Individual Autonomy. *Current Anthropology* 32 (5): 543–572.

Gardner, Peter M. 2014. The Status of Research on South Indian Foragers. *The Eastern Anthropologist* 67 (3/4): 231–255.

Garnsey, Peter and Caroline Humfress 2001. *The Evolution of the Late Antique World*. Cambridge: Orchard Academic.

Geyer, Paul 2007. *Die Entdeckung des modernen Subjekts: Anthropologie von Descartes bis Rousseau*. Würzburg: Königshausen und Neumann.

Giesen, Bernhard and Michael Schmid 1975. System und Evolution: Metatheoretische Vorbemerkungen zu einer soziologischen Evolutionstheorie. *Soziale Welt* 26 (4): 385–413.

Gilbert, Felix 1951. The 'New Diplomacy' of the Eighteenth Century. *World Politics* 4 (1): 1–38.

Gilpin, Robert 1981. *War and Change in World Politics*. Cambridge: Cambridge University Press.

Goddard, Stacey and Daniel H. Nexon 2005. Paradigm Lost? Reassessing Theory of International Politics. *European Journal of International Relations* 11 (1): 9–61.

Godelier, Maurice 1973. Mythos und Geschichte. In: *Die Entstehung von Klassengesellschaften*, edited by Klaus Eder, 301–329. Frankfurt a.M.: Suhrkamp.

Goodall, Jane 1986. *The Chimpanzees of Gombe: Patterns of Behavior*. Cambridge, MA: Harvard University Press.

Gould, Stephen J. 2002. *The Structure of Evolutionary Theory*. Cambridge: Belknap Press.

Gould, Stephen J. and Richard Lewontin 1979. The Spandrels of San Marco and the Panglossian Paradigm: A Critique of the Adaptationist Programme. *Proceedings of the Royal Society B* 205 (1161): 581–598.

Graeber, David and David Wengrow 2021. *The Dawn of Everything*. London: Allen Lane.

Graness, Anke 2017. Der Kampf um den Anfang: Beginnt die Philosophie im Alten Ägypten? *Polylog* 38: 41–62.

Greenwood, Jennifer 2015. *Becoming Human: The Ontogenesis, Metaphysics and Expression of Human Emotionality*. Cambridge, MA: MIT Press.

Gurisch, Simon 2023. *Die Verfassung des Lebens: Die politische Form der Vergesellschaftung durch Individuation bei J. Habermas und G.W.F. Hegel*. Frankfurt a.M.: Ph.D. Dissertation Goethe Universität.

Habermas, Jürgen 1954. *Das Absolute in der Geschichte: Von der Zwiespältigkeit in Schellings Denken*. Bonn: Bonn University.

Habermas, Jürgen 1963. *Theorie und Praxis: Sozialphilosophische Schriften*. Neuwied: Luchterhand.

Habermas, Jürgen 1968. *Erkenntnis und Interesse*. Frankfurt a.M.: Suhrkamp.

Habermas, Jürgen 1976. *Zur Rekonstruktion des Historischen Materialismus*. Frankfurt a.M.: Suhrkamp.

Habermas, Jürgen 1981a. *Theorie des kommunikativen Handelns*. Frankfurt a.M.: Suhrkamp.

Habermas, Jürgen 1981b. Von der Schwierigkeit, Nein zu sagen. In: *Philosophisch-politische Profile*, edited by Jürgen Habermas, 445–452. Frankfurt a.M.: Suhrkamp.

Habermas, Jürgen 1991a. Charles S. Pierce über Kommunikation. In: *Texte und Kontexte*, edited by Jürgen Habermas, 9–33. Frankfurt a.M.: Suhrkamp.

Habermas, Jürgen 1991b. Exkurs: Transzendenz von innen, Transzendenz ins Diesseits. In: *Texte und Kontexte*, edited by Jürgen Habermas, 127–156. Frankfurt a.M: Suhrkamp.

Habermas, Jürgen 1992. *Faktizität und Geltung: Beiträge zur Diskurstheorie des Rechts und des demokratischen Rechtsstaats*. Frankfurt a.M.: Suhrkamp.

Habermas, Jürgen 2004. *Theory of Communicative Action*. Cambridge: Cambridge University Press.

Habermas, Jürgen 2020. *Auch eine Geschichte der Philosophie*. Frankfurt a.M.: Suhrkamp.

Hagedorn, Nancy L. 1988. 'A Friend to Go between Them': The Interpreter as Cultural Broker during Anglo-Iroquois Councils, 1740–70. *Ethnohistory* 35 (1): 60–80.

Haldén, Peter 2020. *Family Power: Kinship, War and Political Order in Eurasia, 500–2018*. Cambridge: Cambridge University Press.

Hampe, Michael 2010. Philosophie. In: *Evolution: Ein interdisziplinäres Handbuch*, edited by Phillip Sarasin and Marianne Sommer, 273–286. Stuttgart: Metzler.

Hauser, Marc D., Noam Chomsky and William Tecumseh Fitch 2002. The Faculty of Language: What Is It, Who Has It, and How Did It Evolve? *Science* 298 (5598): 1569–1579.

Hegel, Georg Wilhelm Friedrich 1952. *Phänomenologie des Geistes*. Hamburg: Meiner.

Hegel, Georg Wilhelm Friedrich 1970. *Enzyklopädie der philosophischen Wissenschaft*. Frankfurt a.M.: Suhrkamp.

Hegel, Georg Wilhelm Friedrich 1975. *Wissenschaft der Logik*. Hamburg: Meiner.

Hegel, Georg Wilhelm Friedrich 1976. *Grundlinien der Philosophie des Rechts oder Naturrecht und Staatswissenschaften im Grundrisse*. Frankfurt a.M.: Suhrkamp.

Hegel, Georg Wilhelm Friedrich 1986. *Vorlesungen über die Philosophie der Geschichte*. Frankfurt a.M.: Suhrkamp.

Heidegger, Martin 1993. *Sein und Zeit*. Tübingen: Niemeyer.

Hirschauer, Stefan 2014. Intersituativität: Teleinteraktionen und Koaktivitäten jenseits von Mikro und Makro. *Zeitschrift für Soziologie* (Special Issue): 109–133.

Hobson, John M. 2012. *The Eurocentric Conception of World Politics: Western International Theory, 1760–2010*. Cambridge: Cambridge University Press.

Horden, Peregrine and Nicholas Purcell 2000. *The Corrupting Sea: A Study in Mediterranean History*. Oxford: Blackwell.

Horkheimer, Max and Theodor W. Adorno 1972. *Dialectic of Enlightenment*. New York: Herder and Herder.

Husserl, Edmund 1976. *Die Krisis der europäischen Wissenschaften und die transzendentale Phänomenologie*. Haag: Nijhoff.

Ikenberry, John 2000. *After Victory: Institutions, Strategic Restraint, and the Rebuilding of Order after Major Wars*. Princeton, NJ: Princeton University Press.

Israel, Jonathan 2014. *Revolutionary Ideas: An Intellectual History of the French Revolution from the Rights of Man to Robespierre*. Princeton, NJ: Princeton University Press.

Jablonka, Eva and Marion J. Lamb 2005. *Evolution in Four Dimensions*. Cambridge, MA: MIT Press.

Jablonka, Eva and Marion J. Lamb 2010. Transgenerational Epigenetic Inheritance. In: *Evolution: The Extended Synthesis*, edited by Massimo Pigliucci and Gerd B. Müller, 137–174. Cambridge, MA: MIT Press.

Jablonka, Eva and Marion J. Lamb 2014. *Evolution in Four Dimensions: Genetic, Epigenetic, Behavioral, and Symbolic Variation*. Cambridge, MA: MIT Press.

Jaeger, Hans-Martin 2014. Governmentality's (Missing) International Dimension and the Promiscuity of German Neoliberalism. *Journal of International Relations and Development* 16 (1): 25–54.

Jaspers, Karl 1949. *Vom Ursprung und Ziel der Geschichte*. München: Piper.

Jaspers, Karl 2021. *The Origin and Goal of History*. London: Routledge.

Jennings, Francis (ed.) 1985. *The History and Culture of Iroquois Diplomacy: An Interdisciplinary Guide to the Treaties of the Six Nations and Their League*. Syracuse, NY: Syracuse University Press.

Johnson, Dominic 2015. Survival of the Disciplines: Is International Relations Fit for the New Millennium? *Millennium: Journal of International Studies* 43 (2): 749–763.

Jung, Dietrich 2022. Abu Hamid al-Ghazali and Niklas Luhmann: Boundary Negotiations between Religion and Science in the Abbasid Empire. *CASHSS Working Paper Series* 26. Leipzig: Leipzig University.

Jung, Dietrich and Stephan Stetter eds. 2018. *Modern Subjectivities in World Society: Global Structures and Local Practices*. New York: Palgrave.

Kaldor, Mary 1999. *New and Old Wars: Organized Violence in a Global Era*. Cambridge: Polity.

Kant, Immanuel 1968. *Kritik der reinen Vernunft*. Berlin: De Guyter.

Kant, Immanuel 1977. *Werke 11: Der Streit der Fakultäten*. Frankfurt a.M.: Suhrkamp.

Kant, Immanuel 1986. *Zum ewigen Frieden: Ein philosophischer Entwurf*. Ditzingen: Reclam.

Khazanov, Anatoly M. and André Wink (eds.) 2001. *Nomads in the Sedentary World*. London: Routledge.

Kierkegaard, Søren 1941. *Tagebücher 1834–1855*. Leipzig: Hegner.

Kierkegaard, Søren 2013. *Entweder/Oder: Ein Lebensfragment*, edited by Victor Eremita. Berlin: Holzinger.

Knauft, Bruce M. 1991. Violence and Sociality in Human Evolution. *Current Anthropology* 32 (4): 391–428.

Knauft, Bruce M. 1994. Reply. In: On Human Egalitarianism: An Evolutionary Product of Machiavellian Status Escalation?, edited by David Erdal and Andrew Whiten, 181–182. *Current Anthropology* 35 (2): 175–183.

Kneer, Georg 1996. *Rationalisierung, Disziplinierung und Differenzierung: Zum Zusammenhang von Sozialtheorie und Zeitdiagnose bei Jürgen Habermas, Michel Foucault und Niklas Luhmann*. Wiesbaden: Westdeutscher Verlag.

Koch, Klaus 1995. *Die Propheten I: Assyrische Zeit*. Stuttgart: Kohlhammer.

Köhn, Rolf 1991. Freiheit als Forderung und Ziel bäuerlichen Widerstandes (Mittel- und Westeuropa, 11.–13. Jahrhundert). In: *Die Abendländische Freiheit vom 10. bis zum 14. Jahrhundert*, edited by Johannes Fried, 325–387. Sigmaringen: Thorbekke.

Koloma Beck, Teresa and Tobias Werron 2018. Violent Conflictitions: Armed Conflicts and Global Competition for Attention and Legitimacy. *International Journal of Politics, Culture, and Society* 31 (1): 275–296.

Koskenniemi, Martti 2001. *The Gentle Civilizer of Nations: The Rise and Fall of International Law 1870–1960*. Cambridge: Cambridge University Press.

Koselleck, Reinhart 2018. *Sediments of Time: On Possible Histories*. Stanford, CA.: Stanford University Press.

Kratochwil, Friedrich 2019. *Praxis: On Acting and Knowing*. Cambridge: Cambridge University Press.

Kuhn, Thomas S. 1962. *Structure of Scientific Revolutions*. Chicago, IL: University of Chicago Press.

Kuntz, Friederike 2018. *Aporias: The International Relation, Interrelated Sovereigns, the Human Individual, and Power-knowledge*. Bielefeld: Ph.D. Dissertation.

Lebow, Richard N. 2013. You Can't Keep a Bad Idea Down: Evolutionary Biology and International Relations. *International Politics Reviews* 1 (1): 2–10.

Lévi-Strauss, Claude 1968. *Das wilde Denken*. Frankfurt a.M.: Suhrkamp.

Lévi-Strauss, Claude 1972. *Vom Honig zur Asche*. Frankfurt a.M.: Suhrkamp.

Lévi-Strauss, Claude 1993. Introduction à l'œuvre de Marcel Mauss. In: *Sociologie et antropologie*, edited by Claude Lévi-Strauss, ix–lii. Paris: Quadrige/PUF.

Linklater, Andrew 2016. *Violence and Civilization in the Western States-System*. Cambridge: Cambridge University Press.

Luhmann, Niklas 1975. Weltgesellschaft. In: *Soziologische Aufklärung*, edited by Niklas Luhmann, 51–71. Opladen: Westdeutscher Verlag.

Luhmann, Niklas 1981. Subjektive Rechte: Zum Umbau des Rechtsbewußtseins für die moderne Gesellschaft. In: *Gesellschaftsstruk-*

tur und Semantik: Studien zur Wissenschaftssoziologie der modernen Gesellschaft, edited by Niklas Luhmann, 45–104, Frankfurt a.M.: Suhrkamp.

Luhmann, Niklas 1995. *Social Systems*. Stanford, CA: Stanford University Press.

Luhmann, Niklas 1997. *Die Gesellschaft der Gesellschaft*. Frankfurt a.M.: Suhrkamp.

Luhmann, Niklas 2000. *Die Politik der Gesellschaft*. Frankfurt a.M.: Suhrkamp.

Luhmann, Niklas 2004. *Law as a Social System*. Oxford: Oxford University Press.

Luhmann, Niklas 2012. *Theory of Society*. Stanford, CA: Stanford University Press.

Luhmann, Niklas 2019. Arbeitsteilung und Moral. In: *Über soziale Arbeitsteilung: Studie über die Organisation höherer Gesellschaften*, edited by Émile Durkheim, 19–38. Frankfurt a.M.: Suhrkamp.

MacGinty, Robert and Oliver P. Richmond 2013. The Local Turn in Peace Building: A Critical Agenda for Peace. *Third World Quarterly* 34 (5), 763–783.

MacKenzie, John M. 2016. Empires in World History: Characteristics, Concepts, and Consequences. In: *The Encyclopedia of Empire*, edited by John M. MacKenzie, lxxxiii–cx. London: Wiley.

Manning, C.A.W. 1962: *The Nature of International Society*. London: Bell & Sons.

Marx, Karl 1904. *A Contribution to the Critique of Political Economy*. Chicago, IL: Charles H. Kerr.

Marx, Karl 1967. *Grundrisse der Kritik der politischen Ökonomie*. Frankfurt a.m.: Europäische Verlagsanstalt.

Marx, Karl 1972. *Kritik der Hegelschen Rechtsphilosophie: Einleitung*. Berlin: Dietz.

Marx, Karl and Friedrich Engels 1974. *Manifest der kommunistischen Partei*. Berlin: Dietz.

Marx, Karl and Friedrich Engels 2010. *Die deutsche Ideologie*. Berlin: Akademie Verlag.

Mattern, Janice B. and Ayşe Zarakol 2016. Hierarchies in World Politics. *International Organization*, 70(3): 623–654.

Maynard Smith, John and Eörs Szathmáry 1995. *The Major Transitions in Evolution*. Oxford: Oxford University Press.

McDermott, Rose and Peter K. Hatemi 2018. To Go Forward, We Must Look Back: The Importance of Evolutionary Psychology for Understanding Modern Politics. *Evolutionary Psychology* 16 (2): 1–7.

McKitrick, Mary C. 1993. Phylogenetic Constraint in Evolutionary Theory: Has It Any Explanatory Power? *Annual Review of Ecology, Evolution, and Systematics* 24 (1): 307–330.

Mercer, Kendrick 2017. *Whole Self: A Concise History of the Birth and Evolution of Human Consciousness*. Hope, ID: The Kendrick Mercer Company.

Merlingen, Michael 2003. Governmentality: Towards a Foucauldian Framework for the Study of IGOs. *Cooperation and Conflict* 38 (4): 361–384.

Messmer, Heinz 2003. *Der soziale Konflikt: Kommunikative Emergenz und systemische Reproduktion*. Stuttgart: Lucius and Lucius.

Meyer, John W. 2000. Globalization Sources and Effects on National States and Societies. *International Sociology* 15 (2): 233–248.

Meyer, John W. and Ronald L. Jepperson 2000. The 'Actors' of Modern Society: The Cultural Construction of Social Agency. *Sociological Theory* 18 (1): 100–120.

Modelski, George and Tessaleno Devezas 2007. Political Globalization is Global Political Evolution. *World Futures* 63 (5/6): 308–223.

Möller, Kolja and Jasmin Siri (eds.) 2016. *Systemtheorie und Gesellschaftskritik: Perspektiven der Kritischen Systemtheorie*. Bielefeld: transcript.

Möller, Kolja 2021. *Volkssouveränität und Gesellschaft. Zur Evolution populistischer Politikformen*. Habilitation thesis, University of Flensburg.

Montefiore, Simon S. 2023. *The World: A Family History of Humanity*. New York: Knopf Doubleday.

Moore, David S. 2015. *The Developing Genome: An Introduction to Behavioral Epigenetics*. Oxford: Oxford University Press.

Moran, William L. 1992. *The Amarna Letters*, edited by William L. Moran. Baltimore, MD: Johns Hopkins University Press.

Morgenthau, Hans 1946. *Scientific Man vs. Power Politics*. Chicago, IL: University of Chicago Press.

Morris, Brian 2014. Anarchism, Individualism, and South Indian Foragers: Memories and Reflections. *The Eastern Anthropology* 67 (3/4): 303–324.

Mouffe, Chantal 1999. Deliberative Democracy or Agonistic Pluralism? *Social Research: An International Quarterly* 66 (3): 745–758.

Muller, Martin M. and Jon C. Mitani 2005. Conflict and Cooperation in Wild Chimpanzees. *Advances in the Study of Behavior* 35 (7/8): 275–331.

Müller, Stephen S.W. 2010. *Theorien sozialer Evolution: Zur Plausibilität darwinistischer Erklärungsansätze sozialen Wandels*. Bielefeld: transcript.

Müller, Thomas and Mathias Albert 2021. Whose Balance? A Constructivist Approach to Balance of Power Politics. *European Journal of International Security* 6 (1): 109–128.

Neumann, Iver B. 2015. Institutionalizing Peace and Reconciliation Diplomacy: Third-Party Reconciliation as Systems Maintenance. In: *Diplomacy and the Making of World Politics*, edited by Ole-Jacob Sending, Vincent Pouliot and Iver B. Neumann, 140–167. Cambridge: Cambridge University Press.

Neumann, Iver B. 2016. Diplomacy: An Evolutionary Perspective. In: *Global Cooperation and the Human Factor in International Relations*, edited by Dirk Messner and Silke Weinlich, 225–245. London: Routledge.

Neumann, Iver B. and Håkon Glørstad 2022. Prehistorical International Relations: How, Why, What. *Global Studies Quarterly* 2 (4): 1–12.

Neumann, Iver B. and Ole Jacob Sending 2010. *Governing the Global Polity: Practices, Mentality, Rationality*. Ann Arbor, MI: University of Michigan Press.

Nietzsche, Friedrich 1980. *Zur Genealogie der Moral. Sämtliche Werke*. München: dtv.

Nicolis, Grégoire and Ilya Prigogine 1987. *Die Erforschung des Komplexen: Auf dem Weg zu einem neuen Verständnis der Naturwissenschaften*. München: Piper.

Numelin, Ragnar 1950. *The Beginnings of Diplomacy: A Sociological Study of Intertribal and International Relations*. Oxford: Oxford University Press.

Olsen, Eckart 1997. Von der Ordnung ohne Recht zum Recht durch Ordnung: Die Entstehung von Rechtsnormen aus evolutionsbiologischer Sicht. In: *Zur Entwicklung von Rechtsbewusstsein*, edited by Ernst J. Lampe, 111–151. Frankfurt a.M.: Suhrkamp.

Osterhammel, Jürgen 2010. *Die Verwandlung der Welt: Eine Geschichte des 19. Jahrhunderts*. München: Beck.

Pape, Helmut 1994. Zur Einführung: Logische und metaphysische Aspekte einer Philosophie der Kreativität: C.S. Peirce als Beispiel. In: *Kreativität und Logik: Charles S. Peirce und das philosophische Problem des Neuen*, edited by Helmut Pape, 6–50. Frankfurt a.M.: Suhrkamp.

Patlagean, Evelyne 1977. *Pauvreté économique et puvreté sociale à Byzanze: 4–7e siècles*. Paris: Mouton.

Peirce, Charles S. 1991. Das Gesetz des Geistes. In: *Naturordnung und Zeichenprozess*, edited by Helmut Pape, 179–210. Frankfurt a.M.: Suhrkamp.

Peña, Alejandro and Thomas Davies 2022. Lateral Relations in World Politics: Rethinking Interactions and Change among Fields, Systems, and Sectors. *International Studies Review* 24 (4), available at: https://doi.org/10.1093/isr/viac048 [accessed 25th February 2023].

Phillips, Andrew and Jason C. Sharman. 2015. Explaining Durable Diversity in International Systems: State, Company and Empire in the Indian Ocean. *International Studies Quarterly* 59 (3): 436–448.

Piaget, Jean 1973. *Das moralische Urteil beim Kinde*. Frankfurt a.M.: Suhrkamp.

Podany, Amanda H. 2010. *Brotherhood of Kings: How International Relations Shaped the Ancient Near East*. New York: Oxford University Press.

Preyer, Gerhard ed. 1998. *Strukturelle Evolution und das Weltsystem*. Frankfurt a.M.: Suhrkamp

Reus-Smit, Christian 1999. *The Moral Purpose of the State: Culture, Social Identity, and Institutional Rationality in International Relations*. Princeton, NJ: Princeton University Press.

Reus-Smit, Christian 2001. *Human Rights and the Social Construction of Sovereignty*. Cambridge: Cambridge University Pres.

Richmond, Oliver P. 2006. *The Transformation of Peace*. Basingstoke: Palgrave.

Riesman, David, Nathan Glazer and Reuel Denney 2020. *The Lonely Crowd: A Study of the Changing American Character*. New Haven, CT: Yale University Press.

Rorty, Richard 1998. *Das kommunistische Manifest 150 Jahre danach*. Frankfurt a.M.: Suhrkamp.

Rosenfield, Israel and Edward Ziff 2018. Epigenetics: The Evolution Revolution. *New York Review of Books*, available at: https://www.nybooks.com/articles/2018/06/07/epigenetics-the-evolution-revolution/ [accessed 10th February 2021].

Rousseau, Jean-Jacques 1971. *Emile oder Über die Erziehung*. Paderborn: Schöningh UTB.

Rousseau, Jean-Jacques 2010. *Constitutional Project for Corsica*. Whitefish: Kessenger Publishing.

Ruggie, John 1986. Continuity and Transformation in the World Polity. *International Organization* 35 (2): 261–285.

Rumelili, Bahar and Lisa Strömbom 2022. Agonistic Recognition as a Remedy for Identity Backlash: Insights from Israel and Turkey. *Third World Quarterly* 43 (6): 1361–1379.

Runciman, Walter G. 1998. The Selectionist Paradigm and its Implications for Sociology. *Sociology* 32 (1): 163–188.

Rüsen, Jörn 2014. Idealism in the German Tradition of Meta-history. In: *The Impact of Idealism: The Legacy of Post-Kantian German Thought*, edited by John Walker, 331–343. Cambridge: Cambridge University Press.

Ryan, Roger 2015. Three Tales of Three Cities in the Book of Judges. *The Expository Times* 126 (12): 578–585.

Salmon, Patrick 2002. Celebrating the First 100 Years of the Nobel Peace Prize. *Security Dialogue* 33 (3): 384–387.

Schecter, Darrow 2019. *Critical Theory and Sociological Theory*. Manchester: Manchester University Press.

Schelling, Friedrich 1946. *Die Weltalter*. München: Biederstein.

Schlichte, Klaus and Stephan Stetter (eds.) 2023. *The Historicity of International Politics: Imperialism and the Presence of the Past*. Cambridge: Cambridge University Press.

Schmid, Michael 1998. Soziologische Evolutionstheorien. In: *Strukturelle Evolution und das Weltsystem*, edited by Gerhard Preyer, 387–411. Frankfurt a.M.: Suhrkamp.

Senghaas, Dieter 1982. *Von Europa lernen: Entwicklungsgeschichtliche Betrachtung*. Frankfurt a.M.: Suhrkamp.

Seth, Sanjay 2011. Postcolonial Theory and the Critique of IR. *Millennium: Journal of International Studies* 40 (1): 167–183.

Sharman, Jason 2014. War, Selection, and Micro-States: Economic and Sociological Perspectives on the International System. *European Journal of International Relations* 21 (1): 194–214.

Shostak, Marjorie 1976. *Nisa: The Life and Words of a !Kung Woman*. Cambridge, MA: Harvard University Press.

Sigrist, Christian 1979. *Regulierte Anarchie. Untersuchungen zum Fehlen und zur Entstehung politischer Herrschaft in segmentären Gesellschaften Afrikas*. Frankfurt a.M.: Syndikat.

Sigrist, Christian 1994. Primärer Sozialismus horizontaler Gesellschaften und etatistischer Sozialismus. In: *Sozialismus in Geschichte und Gegenwart*, edited by Richard Faber, 37–44. Würzburg: Königshausen.

Sivasundaram, Sujit 2020. *Waves Across the South: A New History of Revolution and Empire*. London: Collins.

Spruyt, Hendrik 1994. *The Sovereign State and Its Competitors*. Princeton, NJ: Princeton University Press.

Stäheli, Urs 2000. *Sinnzusammenbrüche: Eine dekonstruktive Lektüre von Niklas Luhmanns Systemtheorie*. Weilerswist: Velbrück.

Stetter, Stephan 2008. *World Society and the Middle East: Reconstructions in Regional Politics*. Basingstoke: Palgrave.

Stetter, Stephan 2014. World Politics and Conflict Systems: The Communication of a 'No' and its Effects. *Horizons of Politics* 12 (1): 43–67.

Stichweh, Rudolf 2002. *Funktionalismus und Evolutionstheorie*, available at: https://www.academia.edu/28334850/Funktionalismus_und_Evolutionstheorie_1990 [accessed 20 March 2023].

Strawson, Peter F. 1962. Freedom and Resentment. *Proceedings of the British Academy* 48: 187–211.

Strawson, Peter F. 1972. *Einzelding und logisches Subjekt*. Stuttgart: Reclam.

Szabó-Bechstein, Brigitte 1991. 'Libertas ecclesiae' vom 12. bis zur Mitte des 13. Jahrhunderts: Verbreitung und Wandel eines Begriffs seit der Prägung durch Gregor VII. In: *Die Abendländische*

Freiheit vom 10. bis zum 14. Jahrhundert, edited by Johannes Fried, 147–177. Sigmaringen: Thorbekke.

Tang, Shiping 2010. Social Evolution of International Politics: From Mearsheimer to Jervis. *European Journal of International Relations* 16 (1): 31–55.

Tang, Shiping 2013. *The Social Evolution of International Politics*. Oxford: Oxford University Press.

Tang, Shiping 2020. *On Social Evolution: Phenomenon and Paradigm*. London: Routledge.

Thayer, Bradley A. 2009. *Darwin and International Relations: On the Evolutionary Origins of War and Ethnic Conflict*. Lexington, KY: University of Kentucky Press.

Thompson, William R. 2001. *Evolutionary Interpretations of World Politics*. London: Routledge.

Thornhill, Christopher 2014. *A Sociology of Constitutions: Constitutions and State Legitimacy in Historical-Sociological Perspective*. Cambridge: Cambridge University Press.

Thornhill, Christopher 2020. *The Sociology of Law and the Global Transformation of Democracy*. Cambridge: Cambridge University Press.

Thornhill, Christopher 2021. *Democratic Crisis and Global Constitutional Law*. Cambridge: Cambridge University Press.

Tierney, Brian 1982. *Religion, Law, and the Growth of Constitutional Thought, 1150–1650*. Cambridge: Cambridge University Press.

Tomasello, Michael 2008. *Origins of Human Communication*. Cambridge, MA: MIT Press.

Tugendhat, Ernst 2007. *Anthropologie statt Metaphysik*. München: Beck.

Uffenheimer, Benjamin 1987. Mythos und Realität im alten Israel. In: *Kulturen der Achsenzeit*, edited by Samuel N. Eisenstadt, 192–239. Frankfurt a.M.: Suhrkamp.

Unger, Roberto and Lee Smolin 2014. *The Singular Universe and the Reality of Time: A Proposal in Natural Philosophy*. Cambridge: Cambridge University Press.

Van de Mieroop, Marc (2016) *A History of the Ancient near East ca. 3000–323 BC*. Chichester: Wiley Blackwell.

von Bogdandy, Armin 2022. *Strukturwandel des öffentlichen Rechts*. Berlin: Suhrkamp.

von Bogdandy, Armin, Matthias Goldmann and Ingo Venzke 2017. From Public International to International Public Law: Translating World Public Opinion into International Public Authority. *European Journal of International Law* 28 (1): 115–145.

Vrba, Elisabeth S. and Stephen J. Gould 1986. The Hierarchical Expansion of Sorting and Selection: Sorting and Selection Cannot be Equated. *Paleobiology* 12 (2): 217–228.

Waltz, Kenneth 1979. *Theory of International Politics*. New York: Random House.

Wartenberg, Gerd 1971. *Logischer Sozialismus: Die Transformation der Kantischen Transzendentalphilosophie durch Charles S. Peirce*. Frankfurt a.M.: Suhrkamp.

Weber, Max 1978. *Gesammelte Aufsätze zur Religionssoziologie I*. Tübingen: Mohr.

Weinfeld, Moshe 1987. Der Protest gegen den Imperialismus in der altisraelischen Prophetie. In: *Kulturen der Aschenzeit*, edited by Samuel N. Eisenstadt, 240–257. Frankfurt a.M.: Suhrkamp.

Wendt, Alexander 1999. *Social Theory of International Relations*. Cambridge: Cambridge University Press.

Wendt, Alexander 2003. Why a World State is Inevitable. *European Journal of International Relations* 9 (4): 491–542.

Wendt, Alexander 2015. *Quantum Mind and Social Science: Unifying Physical and Social Ontology*. Cambridge: Cambridge University Press.

Wilkins, John S. 2008. What's in a Meme? Reflections from the Perspective of the History and Philosophy of Evolutionary Biology. In: *A Mimetics Compendium*, edited by Robert Finkelstein, 1634–1669, available at: https://robotictechnologyinc.com/images/upload/file/-Memetics%20Compendium%205%20February%2009.pdf [accessed 10 February 2021].

Wilson, Michael L. 2012. Long-Term Studies of the Chimpanzees of Gombe National Park, Tanzania. In: *Long-Term Field Studies of Primates*, edited by Peter M. Kappeler and David P. Watts, 357–384. Berlin: Springer.

Wimmer, Hannes 1996. *Evolution der Politik: Von der Stammesgesellschaft zur modernen Demokratie*. Wien: WUV.

Woodburn, James 1982. Egalitarian Societies. *Man, New Series* 17 (3): 431–451.
Yao, Joanne 2022. *The Ideal River: How Control of Nature Shaped the International Order*. Manchester: Manchester University Press.
Zarakol, Ayşe (ed.) 2017. *Hierarchies in World Politics*. Cambridge: Cambridge University Press.